Daily Problems *and* Weekly Puzzlers

grade

6

by

David Yeager

Ideal

Daily Problems *and* Weekly Puzzlers

GRADE 6

David Yeager has more than 15 years of elementary teaching experience in Boulder and Jefferson County, Colorado. In addition to having taught at every grade level from first to seventh grade, he has also served as a teacher on special assignment, as a district curriculum specialist, and as a policy analyst/education aide to the Governor of Colorado.

The author of more than 20 books, articles, and student-teacher materials, David is currently the Director of Development for the Children's Museum of Denver. He also serves as a consultant to several state departments of education. David lives in Boulder, Colorado with his wife Tina, a high school teacher and eight year old son, Christopher.

David holds a bachelor of arts degree from the University of Colorado at Boulder where he earned his Teaching Credential. He has completed graduate work in Education, English, and Technology.

Cover Design: Annelise Palouda
Illustrator: Art Glazer
Text Designer: Violeta Diaz
Art Director: Nancy Tseng
Electronic Production: Joseph Parenteau
Production Coordinator: Theresa Tomlin
Editor and Project Manager: Judy Goodnow

Alsip, Illinois 60482
Printed in U.S.A.
ISBN: 1-56451-198-7
1 2 3 4 5 6 7 8 9 10 . 9 8 7 6 5 6

Table of Contents

Introduction

This book is one of a series of six books for grades 3 through grade 8. This series provides a treasury of challenging and engaging problems from all areas of the math curriculum. The Daily Problems and Weekly Puzzlers are each keyed to the appropriate NCTM Standards, and many of them are designed for "hands-on" problem solving with common classroom manipulatives.

It is a fundamental assertion of the National Council of Teachers of Mathematics (NCTM) that the teaching of mathematics must meet the changing needs of our society. In order to achieve NCTM's goals for becoming more mathematically literate and for developing their mathematical power, this book helps students:

- Learn to value mathematics
- Become confident in their own ability to do mathematics
- Become a mathematical problem solver
- Learn to communicate, using the language of mathematics
- Learn to reason mathematically

Students entering the work force in the twenty-first century will need to have had much practice with thinking and processing information in different ways. Being involved in problem-solving activities helps students develop useful approaches, strategies, techniques, methods, and patterns related to thinking.

Each book contains 144 Daily Problems and 36 Weekly Puzzlers. The Daily Problems are presented four per page, and each one is designed to take students about 15 minutes to solve. The Weekly Puzzlers, which are presented two per page, are more complex problems designed to engage students over a longer period of time and to help them develop a variety of problem-solving strategies. Sample solutions are provided for the problems, many of which have multiple solutions. The chart on page vi lists all of the problems and puzzlers related to each NCTM Standard. Also included is a blackline master for tangram pieces.

Suggestions for Classroom Use

The problems and puzzlers are written for Grade 6, but since ability levels of students vary greatly, you may need to modify the problems to meet the individual needs of your students. For example, you could have your "struggling" students do portions of whole problems, or do them with a partner. You might require your more advanced students to provide more detailed explanations, or to extend the problems and puzzlers in a different way.

One NCTM Standard is referenced for each of the 144 Daily Problems and 36 Weekly Puzzlers. However, you will find that many problems are related to more than one Standard. You can refer to these Standards to help you decide how to use these problems and puzzlers. You may want to focus on one Standard for a week or a month, or you may want to expose students to a variety of Standards over a set period of time. The cross-reference chart for the Standards is designed so that you can choose the problems and puzzlers you want.

The problems and puzzlers may be given to individual students, pairs of students, or small groups. When problem solving, using partners or small-group contexts provides an opportunity for students to share their thinking verbally. Students often are better able to express their thinking in writing after they've had ample opportunities to express their thoughts verbally—a process which helps students articulate, clarify, and modify their ideas.

Many of the Weekly Puzzlers and some of the Daily Problems ask students to extend ideas by writing their own problems. When students have the opportunity to play with operations, algorithms, and numbers, and to create their own problems, they understand the concepts more deeply and personally and can construct their own meaning as they undertake this creative process.

Hints for Using Problems and Puzzlers

- Use as an early morning warm-up. Put one or more problems on the overhead or chalkboard to start your day; then, have "student teacher" volunteers explain their answers to the class.

- Use as homework. Give students a Daily Problem to do each night or a Weekly Puzzler to work on all week.
- Use as a math lab activity. Have teams work on the same problem during a "math lab" period, then take turns explaining the problems to the class. Alternately, you can have student groups work on different problems and rotate the problems as they finish.
- Use in a speed contest. Have a race to see who (or which team) can solve a Daily Problem or Weekly Puzzler the fastest and most accurately.
- Use in an explanation contest (the opposite of a speed contest). Have an "anti-race" to see who (or which group) can best produce a clear and detailed written explanation of a problem or puzzler with no time limit.
- Use as a transformational activity. Have students turn Daily Problems into Weekly Puzzlers, and Weekly Puzzlers into long-term investigations and explorations.
- Use as a quiz. Compile student-created problems into a quiz for everyone to do. Then, correct the quiz together as a whole class so that students can read, answer, and explain their own problems.
- Use as a part of a student's portfolio. Have students select sample Daily Problems and/or Weekly Puzzlers to put in their portfolios and write about why they chose these problems.

Materials Needed

Many of the problems call for the use of manipulatives. We have tried to choose manipulatives that most teachers might have in their classroom. You can use the blackline master for tangram pieces to make paper sets.

Some of the problems specifically call for students to use a calculator. It would be helpful if calculators were available for many of the problems. In some cases students are asked to make estimations first, and then check their estimations using the calculator. Significantly, NCTM Standards recommend that "...calculators should be available to all students at all times." The Standards go on to say, "Contrary to the fears of many, the availability of calculators and computers has expanded students' capability of performing calculations. There is no evidence to suggest that the availability of calculators makes students dependent on them for simple calculations."

Getting Started

Work through a few daily and weekly problems with your class before having the students work independently or in groups. Help students work through a problem, using a problem-solving process such as the following: (1) FIND OUT what the problem means and what question you must answer to solve it; (2) CHOOSE A STRATEGY that will help solve the problem; (3) SOLVE IT using the strategy selected; (4) LOOK BACK or reread the problem and check that solution to see that it meets the conditions stated in the problem.

Model both effective and ineffective problem-solving methods when working with your whole class. In addition, model exemplary and incomplete written explanations, as well as productive and unproductive communication in groups. In this way, you will demonstrate and clarify your expectations for students in either individual or collective problem-solving situations.

Show students how to help each other. Emphasize that giving answers to a partner does not help either student to understand the concepts involved. You can make a game out of this by having the students role-play appropriate and inappropriate ways of interacting with a partner and in a group.

Wrapping Up

Discuss the problems as a class after students complete them. Involve students in the discussion by having them share various problem-solving methods and strategies—allowing everyone to acquire new problem-solving tools. During discussions, it is important to emphasize that many problems in math (and life) have multiple solutions. Seeing a variety of answers to a problem, and hearing how other students reached these different conclusions, underscores the need for students to remain open to more than one path or solution.

Cross-Reference Charts

NCTM Standard	Daily Problem Number	Weekly Puzzler Number
Algebra	4, 13, 22, 31, 40, 58, 67, 76, 85, 93, 101, 109, 116, 144	2, 18, 31
Computation and Estimation	1, 8, 10, 28, 32, 35, 37, 41, 46, 52, 55, 64, 73, 82, 106, 110, 121, 129, 133, 137	1, 12, 21, 24, 25, 29
Geometry	17, 26, 44, 53, 62, 71, 80, 88, 96, 104, 112, 119, 124, 126, 138	3, 9, 14, 28, 32, 34
Logical Reasoning	15, 19, 33, 42, 51, 60, 69, 78, 84, 90, 98, 113, 120, 143	4, 10, 27
Measurement	7, 34, 43, 61, 70, 79, 87, 95, 103, 111, 118, 123, 128, 132, 135, 140	16, 20, 23, 30, 35
Numbers	2, 11, 16, 20, 29, 38, 47, 56, 59, 72, 74, 83, 91, 99, 107, 114, 139	6, 7, 13, 26
Patterns and Functions	3, 6, 12, 21, 25, 30, 48, 57, 66, 75, 92, 100, 108, 115, 122, 127, 130, 134	5, 11, 17
Probability	9, 18, 24, 27, 36, 39, 45, 49, 54, 63, 65, 81, 89, 97, 105, 131, 142	8, 19, 33, 36
Statistics	5, 14, 23, 50, 68, 77, 86, 94, 102, 117, 125, 136, 141	15, 22

Manipulative	Daily Problem Number	Weekly Puzzler Number
Base Ten Blocks	93, 144	
Calculator	4, 7, 8, 10, 11, 12, 13, 16, 19, 25, 28, 29, 32, 33, 34, 35, 37, 40, 41, 43, 44, 46, 47, 48, 52, 55, 59, 64, 67, 73, 76, 91, 92, 95, 103, 106, 110, 111, 116, 118, 120, 121, 127, 128, 129, 130, 133, 135, 137, 139	1, 13, 23, 24, 29, 31
Cards		34
Centimeter rulers	123	
Color Tiles	97, 100, 140	5, 9
Cubes	17, 18, 21, 27, 31, 36, 62, 79, 85, 89, 100, 101, 132	19
Dice	39, 142	1, 25
Geoboard	6, 61, 70, 96, 104, 112	
Geometric solids	126	28
Globe		30
Hundred chart		26
Number lines	12	
Pattern Blocks	63, 80, 119, 122	11
Play money	9	
Spinner	24, 131	
Tangrams	53, 87, 88, 104	14

Solutions

DAILY PROBLEMS

DP 1: 12 (4+3) = 84 or (12 × 3) + (12 × 4) = 84

DP 2: Angelica, Ted, Grace, Ramon, Wilson

DP 3: 2 minutes, 38 seconds

DP 4: Radio: 140,774.16; heating system: $46,924.72; seats: $234,623.60

DP 5: 4.8 miles, 2:1

DP 6: Answers will vary.

DP 7: 2,160 feet; $78.12 each

DP 8: Edgar: 360 pounds per minute; Andrew: 108 pounds per minute

DP 9: 1 in 2; 1 in 4; 1 in 8; 1 in 32; no

DP 10: 33,554,432

DP 11: 3 + 5 + 7 + 11 + 13 + 17 + 19

DP 12: The tire will overinflate Sunday afternoon.

DP 13: Choir: $250; Sports Club: $500; Student Council: $750

DP 14: Answers will vary.

DP 15: A: Valid conclusion; B: There are people *other* than middle school students who like to sleep.

DP 16: Red: 842; blue: 627

DP 17: 2 × 2 × 2: outside-24, inside-24; 3 × 3 × 3: outside-54, inside-108; 4 × 4 × 4: outside-96, inside-288

DP 18: 1 in 39

DP 19: Youngest: 8; triplets: 12; oldest: 16

DP 20: Less than 1. It will keep getting closer to 1.

DP 21: 24

DP 22: 2 hours

DP 23: Answers will vary.

DP 24: Results will vary.

DP 25: Bump 1: 2,250 pounds; Bump 2: 1,687.5; Bump 3: 1,265.6; Bump 4: 929.2; Bump 5: 711.9; Bump 6: 533.9; Bump 7: 400.4; Bump 8: 300.3; Bump 9: 225.2; Bump 10: 168.9 pounds left.

DP 26: 6:00

DP 27: CC, MS, HH; CC, MS, PL; CC, MS, HR; MS, HH, PL; MS, HH, PL; MS, HH, HR. If they choose to do an activity more than once, more combinations are possible.

DP 28: Estimate: 3,000 trips; actual: 3,750

DP 29: Greatest number: Friday (67); fewest number: Thursday (6); total: 128

DP 30: X1112, D1314, W1516, E1718

DP 31: 16 oranges and 5 bananas; 14 oranges and 4 bananas; or 12 oranges and 3 bananas

DP 32: 200 miles

DP 33: A: 48.5 lb; B: 31.9 lb

DP 34: 27,120 seconds

DP 35: Berkeley: 103.5 lb; Dawking: 37.8 lb; Smith: 244.8 lb

DP 36: Most likely one of each; experimental results may vary.

DP 37: $230

DP 38: 30: △ = 13; ○ = 4

DP 39: Julio has a greater chance of getting points: 18 out of 36; Julia's chances are 12 out of 36. The game is unfair.

DP 40: 75: 15 lb, 3 hours 20 min; 80: 16 lb, 3 hours 8 min; 85: 17 lb, 2 hours 57 min; 90: 18 lb, 2 hours 47 min

DP 41: $2,450

DP 42: 16

DP 43: Day 1: 6 miles; Day 2: 10 miles; Day 3: 12 miles; Day 4: 9 miles; Day 5: 15 miles. Total: 4,630; 23 hours, 52 miles

DP 44: 2,700 square feet

DP 45: Answers will vary.

DP 46: 14,850 planks

DP 47: 2,244 total: 459 purple, 459 yellow, 918 red, 306 blue, 102 green

DP 48: $9.75

DP 49: There is a $\frac{3}{16}$ chance of drawing a jester, a $\frac{7}{16}$ chance of drawing an odd number, and a $\frac{9}{16}$ chance of drawing an even number. Experimental results will vary.

DP 50: Answers will vary.

DP 51:

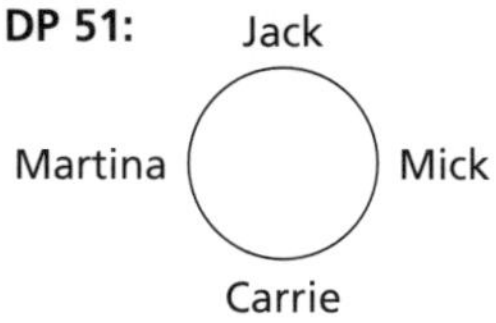

DP 52: 64

DP 53: Answers will vary, but with two sets they can make each shape.

Sample solutions:

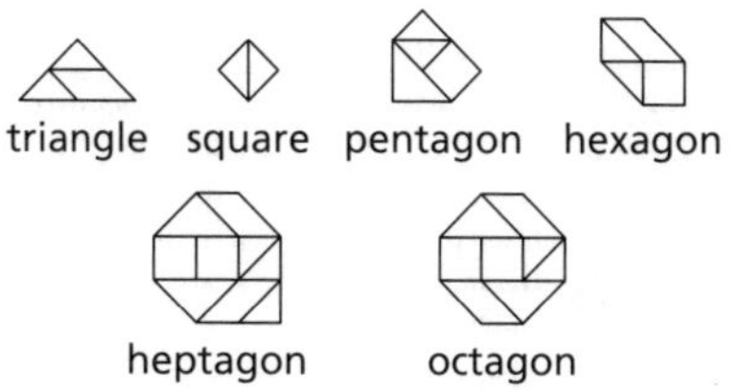

DP 54: One chance in 1,974. No, there is no advantage given the astronomical odds.

DP 55: .01 of a square mile

DP 56: $\frac{1}{5}$, 20%, 1:5

DP 57: 36, .50, .8, 121. Answers may vary; accept any that students can verify.

DP 58: 2B, 7G, 8H, 12M, 15S

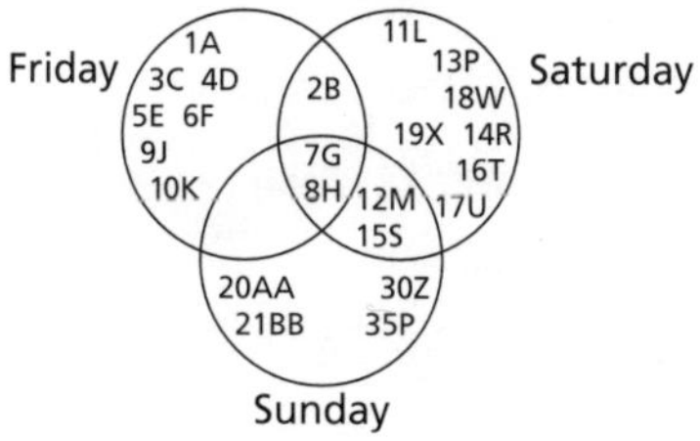

DP 59: 505

DP 60:

	Mountain CLimbing	Bicycles	Rollerblading	Water Skiing	Surfboarding
TJ	Y	N	N	N	N
Babs	N	N	N	Y	N
Ned	N	Y	N	N	N
Glenn	N	N	N	Y	N
Sascha	N	N	N	N	Y

DP 61: Designs will vary.

DP 62: Solutions will vary.

DP 63: Answers will vary.

DP 64: 200 days, 21 miles

DP 65: 120

DP 66: The batteries will no longer work after charge 6.

DP 67: 105 or 140

DP 68:

Order of the members drawing straws. This assumes that the previous person did **not** draw the short straw.	Odds and percentages of drawing the short straw
Mary	1:8 12.5%
Eaglebear	1:7 14%
Devon	1:6 16.5%
Melvin	1:5 20%
Billy Ray	1:4 25%
Angela	1:3 33%
Gretchen	1:2 50%
Doug	1:1 100%

DP 69: 48 in each box: 16 orange, 8 black, 24 white

DP 70: Answers will vary.

DP 71: Baseball

DP 72:

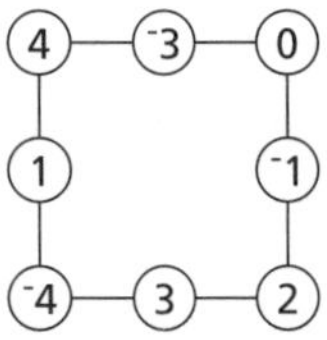

DP 73: 30 cups whole wheat flour, 6 teaspoons salt, 12 teaspoons baking soda, 8 (7.992) cups butter, 8 (7.992) cups honey, 2 dozen eggs, 18 teaspoons vanilla, 19 1/5 cups chocolate chips, 24 cups nuts

DP 74: 107,109

DP 75: 9 offenses, $65.00 fine

DP 76: 72

DP 77: Answers will vary.

DP 78: 6

DP 79: $5 \times 2 \times 2$; $5 \times 4 \times 1$; $10 \times 2 \times 1$; $20 \times 1 \times 1$

DP 80: Solutions will vary.

DP 81: 24

DP 82: 5 times

DP 83: ${}^-6 \times {}^-4$; 8×3; $8 + 16$; $32 + {}^-8$

DP 84: 12 people only have sisters; 8 people only have brothers

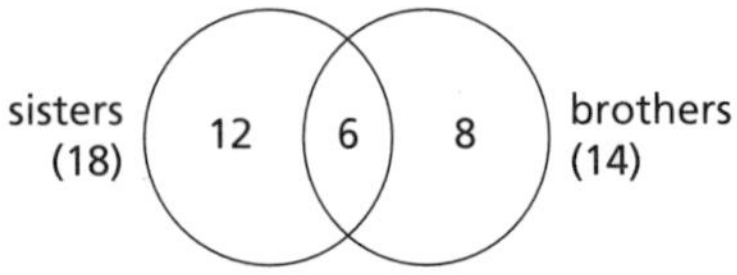

DP 85: $x = 6$; $y + 2x = 22$

DP 86: Median: 7.5; mode: 6; average: 8.14

DP 87: Answers and shapes will vary.

Samples:

6 units 8 units 12 units

DP 88: Solutions will vary.

DP 89: Results will vary.

DP 90: 16

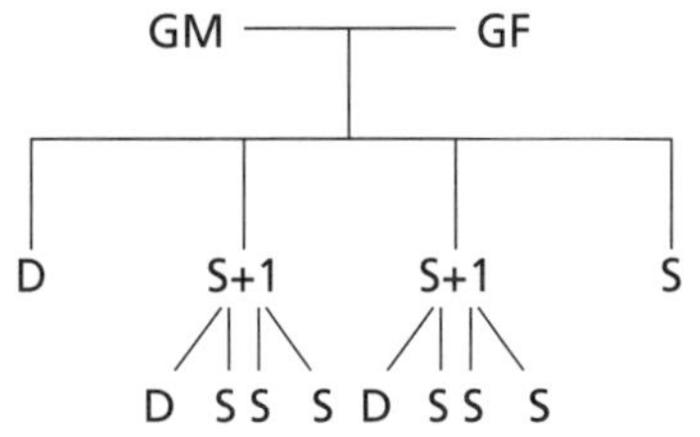

DP 91: 32

DP 92: 17.5 horsepower, 22.5 horsepower, 27.5 horsepower, 16.75 pounds

DP 93: $3x + 6$

DP 94: Answers will vary.

DP 95: 21,937,500 gallons

DP 96: Answers will vary, but the isosceles triangle should touch approximately six pins to be large enough to hold a scalene inside.

DP 97: Answers will vary, unless they specify horizontal line, then 1 out of 6.

DP 98: 7

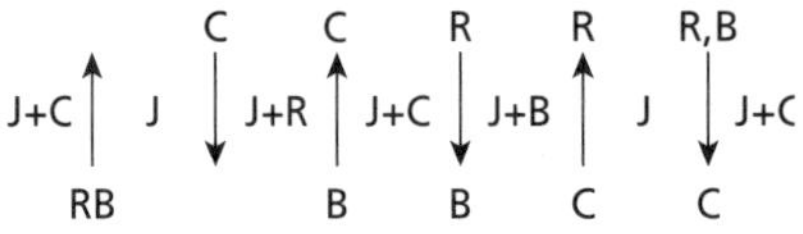

DP 99:

Q	D	N
3	1	2
3	0	4
2	1	7
2	0	9
1	0	14

DP 100: 100 tiles are needed for a 10×10 square; 625 for a 25×25 square. The pattern can be described in several ways: multiply the number of tiles across by the number of tiles down; square the number of tiles on a side; $n \times n$ or n where n^2 is the number of tiles on a side.

DP 101: $b = 4y$; $b = 2y$; $b = \frac{1}{3}y$ or $3b = y$

DP 102: Gymnasium Corridor; reducing; Back Hallway

DP 103: 18.9

DP 104: Both can be formed; solutions will vary.

DP 105: 10, 14 more, 0.8%

DP 106: 28.8, $40.32

DP 107: 13

DP 108: Yes, she does pass the station house.

DP 109: 6, 7, 8, 9, 10, 11, 12, 13

DP 110: Graphs will vary.

DP 111: Approximately 867,532

DP 112: Answers will vary.

DP 113: 9 goats, 12 lambs, 20 rabbits

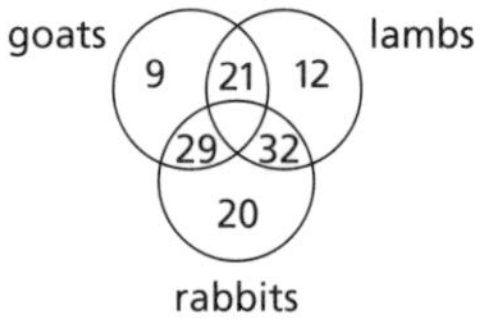

DP 114: 50, 60, 70, 80, 90

DP 115: 675

DP 116: Day 12: 60 Bixies and 50 Hummers. $B = 5n$ and $H = 4n + 2$ where n = the number of the day.

DP 117: Answers will vary.

DP 118: 2

DP 119: Answers will vary, but may include a square, a trapezoid, and a diamond with two acute and two obtuse angles.

DP 120: Centipedes: 455 people; spiders: 160 people

DP 121: Answers will vary; the correct answer is 34,320.

DP 122: 1, 4, 9, 16, 25, 36. Expressions of the rule may vary. Students may notice that the triangles grow in this way: 1 + 3 + 5 + 7 ... and that the series of sums is made up of the square numbers. Students may express the rule as $n \times n$, or n^2, where n is the number of units on the side of the triangle, or the number of the triangle in the series; the 10th triangle will be made of 100 blocks.

DP 123: Answers will vary. Armspan length will probably be similar to height.

DP 124: 2,700 square feet

DP 125: 2

DP 126: Square prism: 4, 6, 8, 12; hexagonal prism: 6, 8, 12, 18. Descriptions of patterns will vary. Students may notice that the number of faces is two more than the number of sides of the base; the number of vertices is two times the number of sides of the base; the number of edges is three times the number of sides of the base.

DP 127: Gregory gets the larger allowance by $2.70.

DP 128: 453,330. He could reduce daily intake by 1,242 calories.

DP 129: Carla and Wilson's: 600 feet; T.C. and Kimiko's: 480 feet

DP 130: 252

DP 131: The spinner could be expected to land on 1 most often. The expected probability is ½, or 50%. Experimental results will vary.

DP 132: 10 cm × 2 cm × 6 cm; or, 4 cm × 5 cm × 6 cm. Other solutions are possible.

DP 133: Katisha: 300, Gretchen: 200

DP 134: It is peace.

DP 135: Mr. Hannigan's offer is best. Under his plan, the kids would be paid 4,000 × 3 square feet × 2 × 0.10 (since there are two sides to a window), equaling $240. Mark's plan pays them 4,000 × 30¢, or $120.

DP 136: 3:1 = ratio of tickets to subscriptions; 3:3 or 1:1 = ratio of refreshments to tickets; 12.5% = money lost

DP 137: 15. You would get a 57½% discount. Answers will vary, but there is a point at which you get a 100% discount.

DP 138: 50.24 feet

DP 139: A: No difference; B: No difference; C: Difference between $^{-}4$ and 4 as dividends; D: No difference

DP 140: A 1 × 60 rectangle has the longest perimeter: 122 units. A 6 × 10 rectangle is 32 units long.

DP 141: Answers will vary.

DP 142: You could expect to roll two even numbers about 5 times in 20. The expected probability is $\frac{9}{36}$, or 25%. Experimental results will vary.

DP 143: Greg: parrot; Iko: dog; Latasha: snake; Ann: cat

	dog	cat	parrot	snake
Peter	N	N	Y	N
Iko	Y	N	N	N
Latasha	N	N	N	Y
Ann	N	Y	N	N

DP 144: 3 Tens, 24 Ones; 6 Tens, 18 Ones

WEEKLY PUZZLERS

WP 1: Answers will vary.

WP 2: $5.25

WP 3: Answers will vary.

WP 4:

001 Enter *x*, the total number of gallons being sold to the customer.

002 If *x* > 4, then skip the next three commands. If *x* < or = 4, proceed to the next line.

003 Multiply *x* by $10.00. The result = *y*.

004 Multiply *y* by 0.07. The result = *z*.

005 Add *y* + *z*. Print the total and end the program.

006 Multiply (*x* − 4) by $7.00. The result = *a*.

007 Add *a* + $40.00. The result = *b*.

008 Multiply *b* by 0.07. The result = *c*.

009 Add *b* + *c*. Print the total and end the program.

WP 5: Answers will vary.

WP 6: Answers will vary.

WP 7: Answers will vary.

WP 8: Answers will vary.

Rome is 42° north of the equator. Miami is about 80° west of Greenwich. Other answers will vary.

WP 9: Answers will vary.

WP 10:

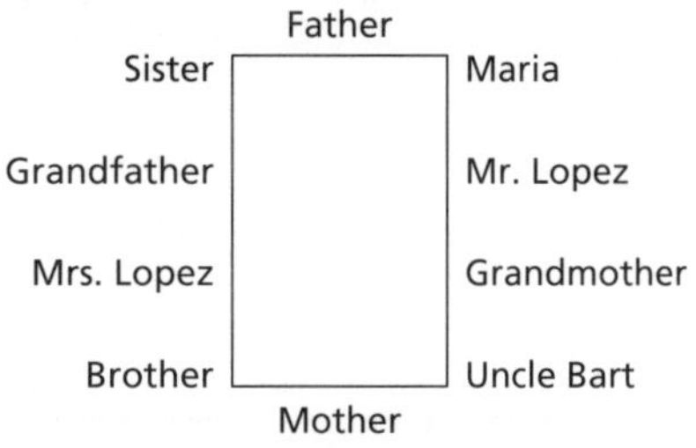

WP 11: The same series of square numbers can be seen for these three kinds of blocks: 1, 4, 9, 16, 25. Descriptions of the patterns will vary.

WP 12: Answers will vary.

WP 13: Twin primes under 100: 3 and 5; 5 and 7; 11 and 13; 17 and 19; 41 and 43; 59 and 61; 71 and 73. One set of triplets: 3, 5, 7

WP 14: Answers will vary.

WP 15: Answers will vary.

WP 16: After 2 moves, 7.5 feet; after 10 moves, 9.99 feet

WP 17: Opposite sectors equal the same number when the numbers are added together.

WP 18: 73.5

WP 19: Answers will vary.

WP 20: Answers will vary.

WP 21: Answers will vary.

WP 22: Answers will vary.

WP 23: Answers will vary.

WP 24: Answers will vary.

WP 25: Answers will vary.

WP 26: Answers will vary.

WP 27: ½ base × height : triangle; dodecahedron : 12; angle < 90° : acute; 2 pints : 1 quart

WP 28: Answers will vary.

WP 29: One possible solution:

8	4	6	5	7
6	7	8	4	5
5	8	4	7	6
4	5	7	6	8
7	6	5	8	4

WP 30: Rome is located about 42 degrees north of the equator; Miami is located about 80 degrees west of Greenwich; other answers will vary.

WP 31: One answer is 260 pounds of cardboard, 250 pounds of newspaper, and 520 pounds of aluminum; many other solutions are possible.

WP 32: Answers will vary.

WP 33: Answers will vary.

WP 34: Answers will vary.

WP 35: Answers will vary.

WP 36: Answers will vary.

Tangram Pieces

Daily Problems

1

Computation and Estimation

Angelica broke her leg skating and must spend the next week in the hospital. Everyone knows how much she loves to read. Twelve people in Angelica's pottery class each brought her three books to read. Twelve players on the school tennis team each brought her four books. How many books did Angelica receive? Show two different ways to write this equation and then solve it using either one.

2

Numbers

Angelica and four of her friends spent the weekend painting the Recreation Room at the Senior Center. Each of them painted a fraction of the room. Who painted the largest area? Put the painters in order.

Angelica: $\frac{2}{7}$ Ramon: $\frac{2}{12}$ Ted: $\frac{2}{9}$

Grace: $\frac{1}{5}$ Wilson: $\frac{1}{8}$

3

Patterns and Functions

Jason is training for the Community 6K Race. He will run a total of 60 blocks during this training run. Jason likes to pace himself during training, changing his speed every five blocks. He begins by running the first five blocks in 15 minutes. He runs the second five blocks in 10 fewer seconds than the first five. He runs the third five blocks in 10 fewer seconds than the second five. If he continues to increase his speed in this way, how long will it take him to run the 60th block?

4

Algebra

Blindar sold three small spacecraft to the Space Force. He didn't give them a very good price, however. He charged extra for the radio, the heating system, and seats. The radio cost three times as much as the heating system, and the heating system cost $\frac{1}{5}$ the price of the seats. The seats were 10% of the total selling price of $2,346,236.00. What was the cost of the radio, the heating system, and the seats?

Daily Problems

5

Statistics

The Sixth Grade Outdoor Education Class is planning a five-day hike along the bay. The map below shows how many miles the students plan to hike each day.

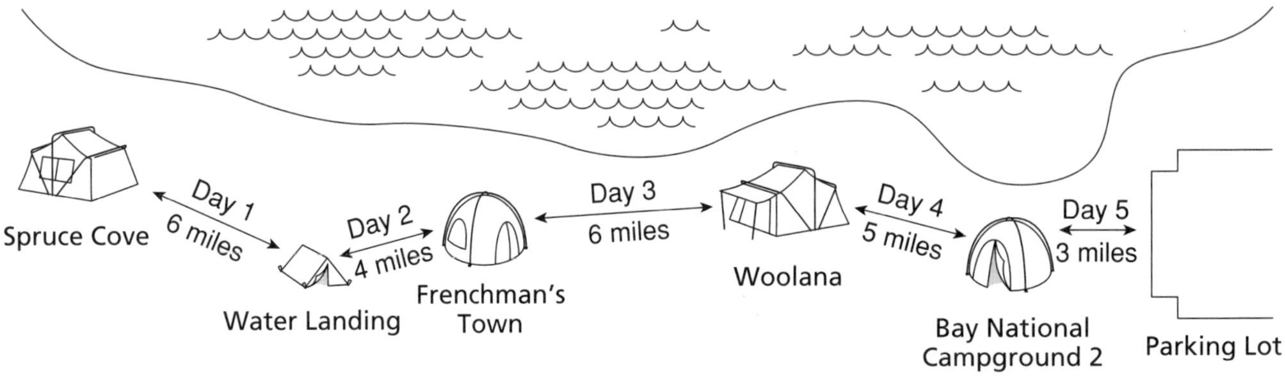

What is the average number of miles the class plans to cover in one day? What is the ratio of miles planned for Day 1 to the number of miles planned for Day 5?

6

Patterns and Functions

Use an 11 × 11-pin geoboard and rubber bands.

Make a square touching eight pins. Now, make another square touching eight pins but let no more than two of those pins be touched by the first rectangle. How many times can you repeat this pattern?

7 

Measurement

The Pep Squad has decided to decorate the gymnasium for the Girls State Basketball Championship. The gym is 60 yards long and 30 yards wide. How many feet of crepe paper will they need to create a red, a white, a blue, and a gold stripe all the way around the gym? How much will each color of crepe paper cost if a five-yard package is $2.17?

8 

Computation and Estimation

Edgar unloads trucks at the lumberyard. His fastest speed for unloading a lumber truck *was* 200 pounds a minute. Last week, when three trucks arrived at the same time, he increased his speed to 180% of his old time. His partner, Andrew, was able to work at just $\frac{3}{10}$ of Edgar's new record. What is Edgar's new record? How many pounds of lumber can Andrew unload a minute?

Daily Problems

9

Probability

Use play coins.

Answer these questions:

- What are the odds that flipping a coin will result in heads?
- What are the odds that two sixth graders, each flipping a coin, will both get heads?
- What are the odds that three sixth graders, each flipping a coin, will all get heads?

Now, have four friends each flip a coin with you. What do you think are the odds that all of you, each flipping a coin, will get heads? Will you ever reach the point where it is impossible for all of you, each flipping a coin, to get heads? What happened when you tried these activities?

10

Computation and Estimation

Blindar is a traveling salesperson from the planet Oralius. This week he is offering Earthlings two Delphi plants for the price of one. Unfortunately, in our atmosphere a Delphi plant becomes a tangled thorn bush that quadruples in number every eight hours. How many Delphi plants will Earth have at the end of 96 hours if Blindar sells just 2 plants?

11

Numbers

Circle the seven prime numbers that, when added together, equal 75.

3, 11, 14, 13, 5, 17, 12, 6, 19, 23, 7, 9

12

Patterns and Functions

Use a number line to chart the changes in tire pressure.

Joshua is having tire trouble with his mountain bike. The tire can hold a maximum of 63 pounds per square inch (PSI) of pressure. Look at this chart of the air pressure in Joshua's tire. If this pattern continues, will the tire eventually be overinflated or become flat? Make an estimate and then find out on what day the tire will be totally overinflated or flat.

Monday a.m.	54 pounds
Monday noon	The tire loses 4 pounds.
Monday p.m.	Josh adds 5 pounds.
Tuesday a.m.	The tire loses 6 pounds.
Tuesday noon	Josh adds 7 pounds.
Tuesday p.m.	The tire loses 8 pounds.
Wednesday a.m.	Josh adds 9 pounds.
Wednesday noon	The tire loses 10 pounds.

Daily Problems

13

Algebra

The Community League donated $1,500.00 to the school to support three student groups: the Choir, the Intramural Sports Club, and the Student Council. The Sports Club spent twice as much as the Choir. The Student Council spent three times as much as the Choir. How much did each club spend?

14

Statistics

The Popmark Popsicle Company is using your class as a test group for its new line of Healthsicles. The graph at the right shows how the class reacted to one flavor.

Use this pie graph to complete the first chart. Based on the chart, estimate how many students fall into each category.

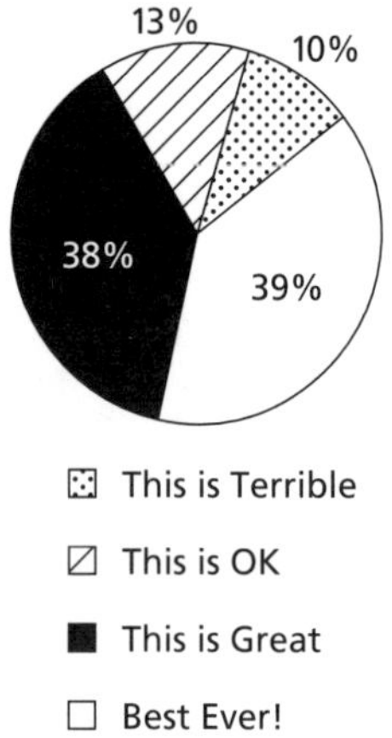

	Terrible	OK	Great	Best Ever
Number of Students				

15

Logical Reasoning

Read each set of statements. Decide whether the statements reach a valid conclusion. Explain why or why not.

A. All birds have feathers.
All pigeons are birds.
Therefore, all pigeons have feathers.

B. All middle school students are humans.
All middle school students like to sleep.
Therefore, everyone who likes to sleep is a middle school student.

16

Numbers

At Mike's Muffins there is a Marble Mystery Jar. If you solve the marble mystery, you win a dozen muffins. Here is the information that is next to the jar:

- There are 1,469 marbles in the jar.
- There are 215 more red marbles than blue marbles.
- How many marbles are there of each color?

Daily Problems

17

Geometry

Use centimeter cubes.

Build each cube shown. How many centimeter-cube faces are on the outside of each cube? How many are hidden inside?

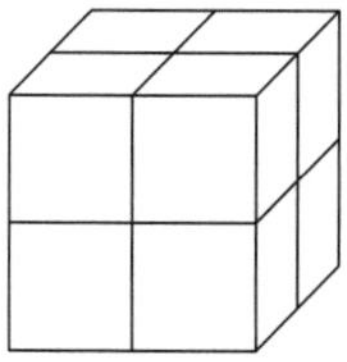

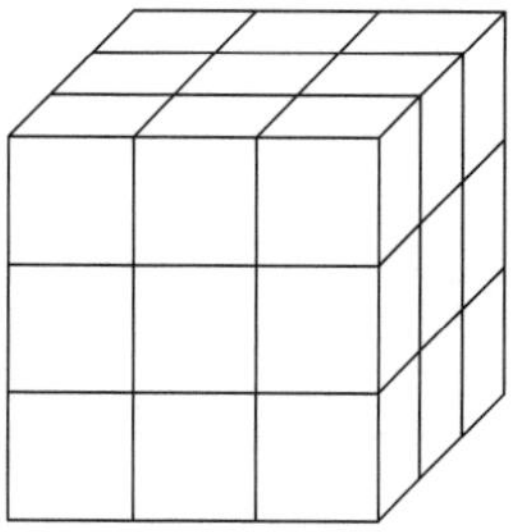

Faces outside ______ inside ______   Faces outside ______ inside ______

Extra challenge: How many faces do you think there are on the outside of the next larger cube? How many faces inside?

18

Probability

Use centimeter cubes and a paper bag.

You have been asked to watch all 20 of Mrs. Googol's kindergarten students on the playground. Before you can stop them, every one of them has thrown both shoes down the storm drain where you can't see them. Using a stick, you pull the shoes out one at a time. What are the odds that the second shoe you pull up will match the first? Predict. Then test your prediction by putting cubes in the bag and drawing them out one at a time. Record your results.

19 

Logical Reasoning

There are five children in the Lopez family. The youngest is in third grade. The oldest is twice as old as the youngest. The triplets are four years younger than the oldest. The product of all the children's ages is 221,184. How old is each child?

20

Numbers

Begin with the fraction $\frac{1}{2}$. Make a new fraction by doubling the denominator and keeping 1 for the numerator. Do this again, so you have:

$$\frac{1}{2} + \frac{1}{4} + \frac{1}{8} +$$

Continue this pattern with two more fractions. Do you think the sum of these fractions will be greater than or less than 1? Find the answer. What do you think will happen when you repeat this 10 times? 20 times?

Daily Problems

21

Patterns and Functions

Use Color Cubes.

The Smiths are moving across town. Four of Angelica's friends—Ron, Juan, Don, and Connie—have agreed to help Angelica load her furniture onto the truck. The four friends form a line from the truck to Angelica's room and begin passing furniture from one to another. How many different ways can they line up?

22

Algebra

Melvin and Warren agreed to start a handyman's service. They planned to work on six projects over the long weekend. They estimated that each job would take a certain amount of time. To their surprise, each job took three times that long. If the total time spent on the projects was 36 hours, and if each job took the same amount of time, what was their estimate of how long each job would take?

23

Statistics

This graph shows the individual heights of the 20 clowns who work for the Bluebird and Bunny Kiddie Circus.

What does the information tell you about the clowns who work for the Bluebird and Bunny Kiddie Circus? List at least three facts.

1.

2.

3.

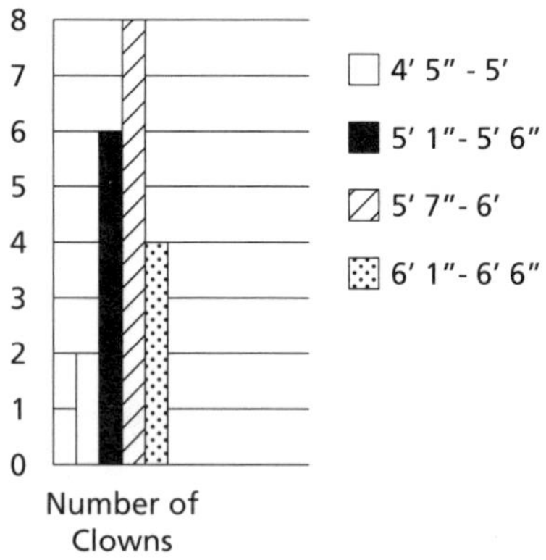

24

Probability

Make a spinner like the one shown. Put a pencil in the center, holding a paper clip. Spin the paper clip.

Before spinning, predict where the pointer will stop. Write your prediction in column 1. In column 2, write the probability that you will be correct. Then spin until your prediction comes true. In column 3, record the number of times you had to spin before your prediction came true. Try this several times. Are you pretty good at guessing the correct spot?

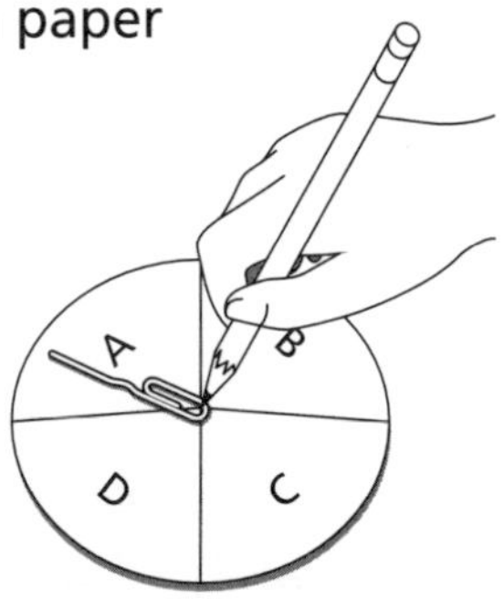

Prediction	Probability	Spins Needed

Daily Problems

25

Patterns and Functions

McKenzie's Delivery Service has been having a terrible time with the doors on their largest truck. They started the morning with a full load of 3,000 pounds. Each time they went over a bump, they lost 25% of the load that was still on the truck. Make a "bump" line to chart the diminishing weight in the back of the truck. Round all of your figures to the nearest tenth.

26

Geometry

Blindar never has quite understood Earth time. When someone asked him what time it was he replied, "180 degrees." What time was it?

27

Probability

You may want to use centimeter cubes to work out this problem.

It's Party Day at the zoo. Gina and her friends each have three tickets, so they are trying to decide what three activities they want to do. They could enter a costume contest, watch a monkey show, go through a haunted house, watch a play, or go on a hay ride. What are the different combinations of three activities they could choose?

28

Computation and Estimation

At one time, 30,000 Americans held reservations on Pan American Airline's first flights to the moon. If the space shuttle—the only way now to fly even close to the moon—can seat only eight people comfortably, estimate the number of trips Pan Am would have to make to serve all of the customers with reservations for flights to the moon—*if* Pan Am owned a shuttle and *if* they had not gone out of business several years ago.

Daily Problems

29

Numbers

Ben and Amy collected this number of cans during the week:

Monday: A prime number that is < 20 and > 17.
Tuesday: A number that is the square of 4.
Wednesday: A number that is the greatest common factor (GCF) of 20 and 40.
Thursday: The GCF of 54 and 60.
Friday: A prime number > 62 and < 70.

On which day did they collect the greatest number of cans? On which day did they collect the fewest number of cans? How many cans did they collect altogether?

30

Patterns and Functions

Tickets 2000 prints and sells concert tickets. Each ticket carries a serial number to avoid counterfeiting. Look at the numbers on the tickets and fill in the serial numbers on the last tickets for the hottest band of the year.

A1002	Z3004	B5006	Y7008	________	________
________	________	________			

31

Algebra

Use centimeter cubes.

Minna ran an errand for her neighbor. She went to the store and bought two dozen pieces of fruit. She purchased three times as many oranges as bananas. On her way home she dropped twice as many oranges as bananas, but still managed to deliver more than a dozen pieces of fruit to her neighbor. What did she deliver?

32

Computation and Estimation

Modern hot-air balloons burn propane to stay afloat. The average balloon carries 60 gallons of propane and burns about 15% of it each hour. If a hot-air balloon catches a good wind, it can travel about 30 miles in an hour. How far can a balloon travel with a good wind and a full load of propane before it has to set down to refill its tanks?

Daily Problems

33

Logical Reasoning

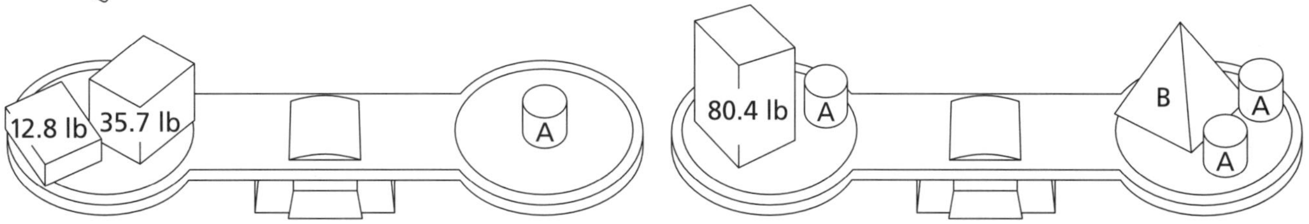

What do A and B each weigh?

34

Measurement

J.J., Greg's younger brother, has decided to measure everything he does in seconds. If he is in school for 7 hours and 32 minutes, how many seconds is he there? Do you think that measuring everything in seconds will make time seem to move more quickly or more slowly?

35

Computation and Estimation

Twenty-five hundred people attended the all-school carnival. The sixth grade was asked to clean up the trash left behind. Find out which sixth-grade class had the best trash collectors: Mrs. Berkeley's class collected 3 times the amount minus 9.9 pounds as that collected by Mr. Dawking's; Mr. Dawking's class collected 56 pounds, but then lost 10% of it when a large bag broke, and then lost $\frac{1}{4}$ of the rest when Sasha tripped while carrying a bag to the dumpster; and Ms. Washington's class picked up all the trash Sasha dropped and added it to their collection, which was already twice as large as Mrs. Berkeley's. How many pounds of trash did each class collect?

36

Probability

Use centimeter cubes and a paper bag. Work with a partner if you can.

Chancy the Clown is giving out pogs and ride tokens at the county fair. There are 10 pogs and 10 ride tokens in her pocket. If Chancy pulls two prizes out of her pocket, are they most likely to be two pogs, two tokens, or one of each? Predict.

Now try it. Choose two colors of cubes—one for pogs and the other for ride tokens. Put 10 of each color into the bag. Without looking, draw two cubes out of the bag. Record your results, then put the cubes back into the bag. Do this 20 times in all. Compare your results with your prediction.

Daily Problems

37

Computation and Estimation

The Hockey Club is going to play in a national tournament. Each of the 23 players in the club practices 4 hours on Saturday, 6 hours on Sunday, and $\frac{1}{5}$ of the total weekend time each weekday afternoon. If the ice skating arena charges the club 50¢ a member per hour to practice, how much does the club spend a week on "ice time"?

38

Numbers

Hikers in a remote area found some interesting writing on cliff walls. On the first wall were these symbols:

△ ○

which represented the number 17. On the second wall were these symbols:

△ △ △ ○ ○ ○

which represented the number 51. On the third wall the hikers found this:

△ △ ○

What number did these last symbols represent?

39

Probability

Use two regular dice, each numbered 1-6.

Julio and Julia are playing a game with the dice. They roll both dice and then subtract the smaller number from the larger number. Julio gets 10 points for each answer that is an odd number and Julia gets 10 points for each answer that is an even number. Is this game fair? Why or why not? If it is not fair, how would you change the rules?

40

Algebra

The Science Club built a car that operates on melting ice. The car holds one 50-pound block of ice. The ice melts at a rate of 2 pounds per hour for every 10 degrees of temperature. How long will the ice last at the temperatures shown in the table?

Temperature	Pounds Melted Per Hour	Time Ice Lasts
70°	14	3 hours 34 minutes
75°		
80°		
85°		
90°		

Daily Problems

41

Computation and Estimation

A ton of $5.00 bills is worth a whopping $4,900,000.00. Knowing this, can you determine the value of a *pound* of $5.00 bills?

42

Logical Reasoning

Harriet is helping out at Morning Glory Preschool. At noon she noticed that $\frac{1}{2}$ of the children were missing. When she called, $\frac{1}{2}$ of the missing children returned to the room. But as soon as Harriet turned her back, $\frac{1}{2}$ of the children in the room left again. Of those who stayed in the room, $\frac{1}{2}$ played with the blocks, $\frac{1}{3}$ started to paint, and the rest fell asleep. If just one child is sleeping, how many children are in the class?

43

Measurement

The Outdoor Education Class is on a five-day hike. Each day that the hike involves an elevation gain of more than 5,000 feet, the students walk 1.5 miles an hour. Each day that there is an elevation gain of 5,000 feet or less, the students average 2 miles an hour. Each day that there is an elevation loss, the class covers 3 miles an hour. Before completing the table below, estimate in your mind the number of miles the students will hike during the five days. Then complete the table and see how close your estimate is to the actual distance.

My estimate:

Day	Elevation Gain/Loss	Hours They Hiked	Distance They Covered
1	+6,420	4	
2	+310	5	
3	+5,000	6	
4	-100	3	
5	-7,000	5	
Total			

44

Geometry

The Summer Community Kids invented a new game that involves football, soccer, and water balloons. The playing field is 180 yards long but only 5 feet wide. What is the total area of this unusual playing field?

Daily Problems

45

Probability

Some things are more predictable than others. Which of the following can you *not* easily determine the probability of?

A. That you will accidentally trip while walking to your next class.
B. That when rolling two dice, two numbers that can add up to six appear face up.
C. That you will climb Mount Everest after school.
D. That at least one baby born within the next hour will be named Harold.
E. That you will be invited to sing the national anthem at the World Series.

46

Computation and Estimation

The Service Club is building a boardwalk hiking trail for people with disabilities. The completed trail will be 2.5 miles long and built of 2 inch-deep by 4 inch-wide by 8 inch-long weather-resistant planks laid end to end. If the walkway is 9 planks wide, how many $2 \times 4 \times 8$ planks will be needed to complete the job? There is an old expression among carpenters: "Measure twice and cut once."

47

Numbers

Al and Anita work at Party Animals. They were asked to blow up animal balloons for a big party. When they finished, they were supposed to have the same number of purple and yellow balloons, $\frac{1}{2}$ as many yellow balloons as red balloons, three times as many red balloons as blue balloons, and three times as many blue balloons as green balloons. They had to blow up 102 green balloons. How many balloons did they have to blow up? How many of each color?

48

Patterns and Functions

Everything, it seems, is showing up on trading cards. And some of the cards get more and more valuable with age, as J.T. recently discovered. She was about to throw away her collection of Super- Mutant Hero cards when she saw this advertisement in the paper:

WANTED

Old trading cards. Will pay top dollar.
Five-year-old cards: $1.00 each
Six-year-old cards: $1.50 each
Seven-year-old cards: $2.25 each
Eight-year-old cards: $3.25 each

If this pattern continued, how much would a 12-year-old Super-Mutant card be worth?

Daily Problems

49

Probability

Use a sheet of construction paper, scissors, and crayons. Work with a partner if you can.

Fold the paper to make 16 game cards of equal size. Cut the cards apart. Draw pictures of jokers on three cards and number the remaining cards 1 through 13. Shuffle the cards and lay them face down on a draw pile.

If you take the top card from the pile, what do you predict you will get: an even number, an odd number, or a joker? Try it. Take a card from the top of the pile and record what you get. Put the card into the pile and shuffle the cards. Draw again. Do this 20 times. Compare your results with your prediction.

50

Statistics

What's the frequency? Ask 10 of your friends the last digit of their telephone number. Record each occurrence with a tally mark in the middle column. Create a frequency distribution by answering the questions that follow:

What number occurs most frequently? What number occurs least frequently?

Try this again with 10 other friends. How do the results differ?

Number	Tally	Total
0		
1		
2		
3		
4		
5		
6		
7		
8		
9		

51

Logical Reasoning

Jack, his sister Carrie, Mick, and Martina are playing a game at Mick's kitchen table. Use these clues and a diagram to decide where each person is sitting. Everyone sits facing the table.

- Jack is not sitting next to his sister.
- Mick is sitting to the right of Carrie's brother's partner.

52

Computation and Estimation

Brad has agreed to take over his brother's paper route while his brother is out of town. Brad's mother drives while Brad throws the papers. Out of a total route of 320 papers, Brad missed four times the number of front door areas as he hit. How many papers landed at the front door?

Daily Problems

53

Geometry

Use two sets of tangrams.

Can you make each of these shapes? In the table, list the number of tangram pieces you used.

Shape	Number of Sides	Number of Pieces Used to Make the Polygon
A. Triangle		
B. Square		
C. Pentagon		
D. Hexagon		
E. Heptagon		
F. Octagon		

54

Probability

Riverside Mall is holding its annual Midnight Mall Mayfest Contest. Twenty-five people, including Angela, have won the chance to reach into the Pirate's Chest and pull out the key to the mall. There are 14 keys in the chest along with 860 key-shaped pretzels, 500 plastic key rings, and 600 five-dollar gift certificates folded into small metal tubes. What are the odds that Angela will reach in and pull out a key? Given the number of prizes in the pirate's chest, is there a statistical advantage in going first rather than twenty-fifth?

55 

Computation and Estimation

The United States is the fourth-largest country in the world, with 3,614,170 square miles of land. In 1990, the population of the country was 250,942,000 people. If all those people agreed to divide the land evenly among themselves, how much land would each person get? Round to the nearest hundredth. Double-check your answer.

56

Numbers

Jason collects pennies in a five-gallon water bottle. He has 860 pennies in the bottle. Six hundred and eighty-eight of the pennies were minted in 1970 or later. Express the portion of the pennies that were minted before 1970 as a lowest-term fraction, a percentage, and a ratio.

Daily Problems

57

Patterns and Functions

Complete these pattern analogies:

5 is to 25 as 6 is to _____

$\frac{1}{4}$ is to $\frac{1}{2}$ as 0.25 is to _____

$\frac{1}{5}$ is to $\frac{4}{5}$ as 0.2 is to _____

7 is to 77 as 11 is to _____

58

Algebra

The sixth grade is using the faculty parking lot to park cars this weekend for the Community Festival. Each car is given a parking pass with a number on it. Angela sold parking permits for 10 cars for Friday, 12 cars for Saturday, and 9 cars for Sunday. Create a Venn diagram that shows which cars used the lot more than once.

Friday: 1A 2B 3C 4D 5E 6F 7G 8H 9J 10K

Saturday: 11L 12M 2B 13P 18W 19X 7G 8H 14R 15S 16T 17U

Sunday: 7G 12M 20AA 21BB 8H 13P 30Z 35P 15S

59

Numbers

I'm a three-digit palindrome.

The product of my digits is divisible by five.

Who am I?

Make your own Mystery Number problem for another three-digit palindrome.

60

Logical Reasoning

The kids on Maple Avenue (T.J., Babs, Ned, Glenn, and Sascha) each have a favorite sport. The sports are roller blading, mountain climbing, surfing, biking, and water skiing. Make a chart and use the following clues to help solve the problem.

- T. J.'s boots always give him blisters.
- When Babs goes to school, she goes almost as fast as the kids on bikes.
- Ned hates getting wet.
- Glen goes to the lake every weekend with his grandfather, who has a powerboat.

Daily Problems

61

Measurement

Use a geoboard and rubber bands.

Make five different shapes that each have a perimeter 12 units long. Draw the shapes. Do your shapes have the same area?

62

Geometry

Use centimeter cubes and a piece of cardboard.

Look at these three views of a building.

Use the cubes to construct the building on the cardboard. Turn your building around to see whether it matches the front and side views. Then look down on your building to see whether it matches the top view.

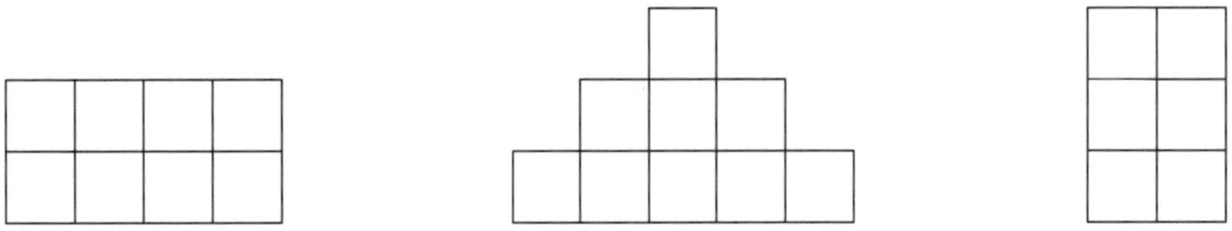

top view   front view   side view

Design your own building. Draw three views of it. Let a partner try to make your building by looking at your views.

63

Probability

Use Pattern Blocks and a paper bag.

Place six each of three different-shaped blocks into a bag. Pull out three blocks, one at a time, and place them on the table from left to right. If you draw three blocks from the bag again, what is the chance that you will repeat this pattern exactly? Make your prediction. Then see if it is right.

64 

Computation and Estimation

The Nile is the longest river in the world, flowing 4,145 miles through Africa to the Mediterranean Sea. If you dropped a model boat in the water where the river begins and it floated $\frac{1}{2}$% of the total distance to the sea each day, how long would it take for your model to reach the end of the Nile? How far would it float each day? Round the distance to the nearest whole number.

Daily Problems

65

Probability

The Booster Club has designed five school-spirit flags that can be waved during sporting events. How many different ways can the flags be arranged along the sidelines?

66

Patterns and Functions

Tyrone has developed a combination radio, CD player, television, cellular phone, and game player that fits in the palm of his hand. Unfortunately, the batteries needed to power the thing are huge and don't last long. When the batteries are new, they last four hours before they need to be recharged. After the first charge, they last only 3.8 hours. After the second charge, they last just 3.4 hours, and after the third charge just 2.8 hours. What will eventually happen to the batteries? When will that occur?

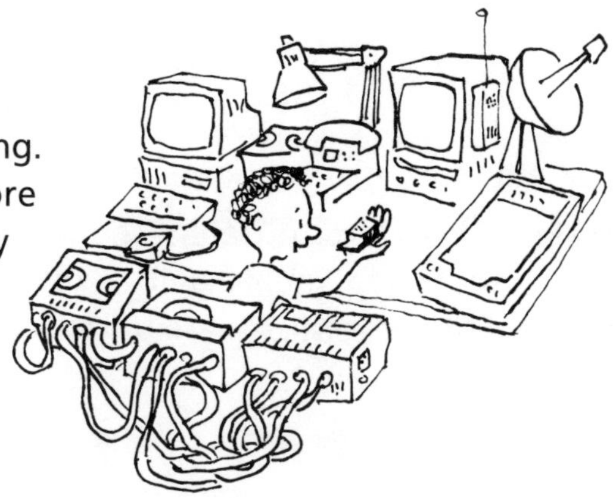

67

Algebra

What is the Mystery Number?

It is less than 150 and greater than 100.
It is divisible by 7 and by 5.

68

Statistics

The Environmental Club has collected 100 pounds of scrap aluminum for the Community Center recycling drive. One of the eight members of the club has to crush each can. The members decide to draw straws to see who is unlucky enough to get the job. List the odds of each person in the club drawing the short straw.

Order of the members drawing straws. This assumes that the person before did *not* draw the short straw.	Odds and percentage of drawing the short straw
Mary	
Eaglebear	
Devon	
Melvon	
Billy Ray	
Angela	
Gretchen	
Doug	

Daily Problems

69

Logical Reasoning

Boris works at Halloween Horrors. He puts orange, black, and white Halloween candies in boxes. After he fills a box, $\frac{1}{3}$ is orange, $\frac{1}{6}$ is black, and 24 are white. How many candies does Boris put in each box? How many of each color? Hint: A diagram can help solve the problem.

70

Measurement

Use a geoboard and rubber bands.

Make at least four different shapes on the geoboard. Each should have a total area equal to six square units. Explain how you know that the area of each shape is equal to six square units.

71

Geometry

How much space do you need to play?

A regulation basketball floor is 94 feet by 50 feet.

A regulation baseball diamond is 90 feet on a side.

A regulation volleyball court is 30 yards by 15 yards.

Which sport requires the greatest area?

72

Numbers

Fill in the Magic Square so that each side has a sum of 1. Use these integers: 0, 1, $^{-}1$, 2, 3, $^{-}3$, 4, $^{-}4$.

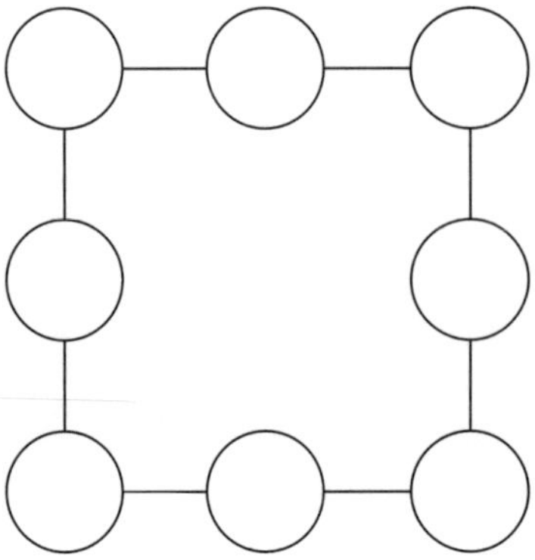

Daily Problems

73

Computation and Estimation

The Parents Club has decided to bake cookies shaped like tennis and field-hockey balls to support those teams. The recipe for five dozen round carob cookies is:

$1\frac{1}{4}$ cups whole wheat flour
$\frac{1}{4}$ teaspoon salt
$\frac{1}{2}$ teaspoon baking soda
$\frac{1}{3}$ cup butter
$\frac{1}{3}$ cup honey
1 egg
$\frac{3}{4}$ teaspoon vanilla
$\frac{4}{5}$ cup chocolate chips
1 cup chopped nuts

What quantity of each ingredient will the Parents Club have to buy to bake 1,440 cookies?

74

Numbers

What are the Mystery Numbers?

We are twin primes.

We are greater than 100 and less than 200.

The product of the sum of the digits of the first number times the sum of the digits of the second number is 80.

Note: Twin primes are pairs of prime numbers that have a difference of two.

75

Patterns and Functions

The City of East Cove has a dog-at-large problem. Last week, the town council passed a tough new law. The first time a dog is picked up running at large, the owner must pay a \$25.00 fine and spend two hours cleaning the town's parks. Each repeat offense carries a \$5.00 increase in the fine and an additional $\frac{1}{2}$ hour cleaning the parks. If Jim must now spend six hours cleaning the park, how many times has his dog been caught without a leash and how much is the current fine?

76

Algebra

Mr. Simms formed three problem-solving teams in his class. Each team was asked to bring three colored markers, four times the number of rulers as markers, and twice the number of sheets of graph paper as rulers. How many sheets of paper did the class bring altogether?

Daily Problems

77

Statistics

Pick a sentence that you wrote sometime during the day. Create a frequency chart that shows how often each letter of the alphabet was used in your sentence. Then, compare your frequency chart with ones that your classmates made. Which letters appear most frequently? Which appear least frequently?

78

Logical Reasoning

Begin with the number 1,234. Rearrange two adjacent numbers at a time. What is the fewest number of steps it will take before you can write the number 4,321?

79

Measurement

Use centimeter cubes.

How many different rectangular prisms can you build using 20 cubes for each one? Record the length, width, and height of each rectangular prism.

Volume (cubic units)	Length (units)	Width (units)	Height (units)
20	5		
20			
20			

80

Geometry

Use Pattern Blocks, a blank sheet of paper, and colored pencils or markers.

Choose two or three kinds of blocks. Using only those kinds of blocks, try to fill the space on the paper without gaps or overlaps. (It's okay if the blocks go beyond the edges of the paper.) If the blocks do not fill the space, try other combinations of blocks. When you find a combination that makes a repeating design which fills the space, trace the blocks and color the spaces.

Daily Problems

81

Probability

Mr. Blackwelder is teaching his students about probability. He pulls four cards from a bag. On each of the cards a number is written:

4	6	0	1

How many different four-digit numbers can be formed from the four numbers using each numeral only once?

82

Computation and Estimation

The hit movie of the summer is "My Neighbor Is from Neptune," a science fiction comedy. If the theater the movie plays at opens at 10:00 a.m. and closes at 10:00 p.m., and the clean-up crew needs 30 minutes after each showing to clean the floor, how many times can the 105-minute film be shown in a day?

83

Numbers

Use the following numbers to make the four equations each equal 24.

$-8, -6, -4, 3, 8, 8, 16, 32$

$\_\_\_\_ \times \_\_\_\_ = 24$

$\_\_\_\_ \times \_\_\_\_ = 24$

$\_\_\_\_ + \_\_\_\_ = 24$

$\_\_\_\_ + \_\_\_\_ = 24$

84

Logical Reasoning

Leah is doing a survey to see how many people have sisters and how many people have brothers. Out of 26 people that she talked to, 18 have sisters, 14 have brothers, and 6 have both sisters and brothers. How many people have *only* sisters and how many people have *only* brothers?

Hint: Use a Venn diagram to help solve this problem.

Daily Problems

85

Algebra

Use centimeter cubes.

If y represents 10 yellow cubes and x represents the number of red cubes, how many red cubes does x stand for in the following equation:

$y - x = 4$

Using that value of x, what is the solution for this equation?

$y + 2x =$

Make some equations of your own using $x = 10$ red cubes.

86

Statistics

This table shows the number of rebounds Melanie had during her season with the basketball team. What are the median, mode, and average number of rebounds she had for the season?

Game	1	2	3	4	5	6	7	8	9	10	11	12	13	14
Rebounds	8	7	6	9	4	7	9	8	10	12	6	4	18	6

Median:

Mode:

Average:

87

Measurement

Use one set of tangram pieces.

Assume that the small triangle has two units of area. Create shapes that have 6 units of area, 8 units of area, and 12 units of area. Trace the shapes and label them with the units of area.

88

Geometry

Use two sets of tangram pieces, blank paper, and scissors.

Here are two shapes that you can make by putting two small triangles together. One shape has one line of symmetry and one shape has four lines of symmetry. If you fold a shape along a line of symmetry, one half of the shape fits exactly onto the other half.

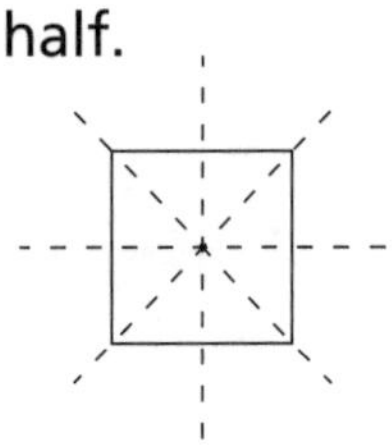

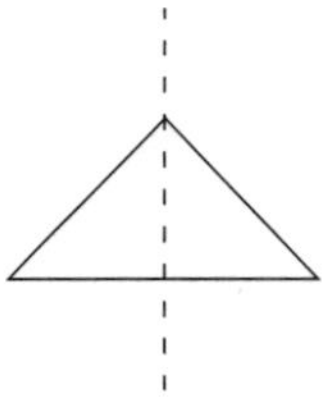

Use tangram pieces to make five other shapes that have lines of symmetry. Trace them, cut them out, and fold them to check.

Daily Problems

89

Probability

Use centimeter cubes and a paper bag. Work with a partner if you can.

Choose three colors of cubes: A ________ B ________ C ________

Put cubes into the bag to fit these conditions:

- The chance of drawing color A is the same as the chance of drawing color B.
- The chance of drawing color C is greater than the chance of drawing color A.

Now experiment. Draw one cube from the bag without looking. Record the color. Put the cube back into the bag. Keep drawing for a total of 20 times. Do your results almost match the conditions shown above?

90

Logical Reasoning

In the Akimoto family there is one grandmother, one grandfather, and three fathers. Each father has one daughter. Each daughter has three brothers. Each grandchild has one aunt and two uncles. What is the fewest number of people that could be in the Akimoto family? Hint: Use a diagram to help solve this problem.

91 

Numbers

Which of the following numbers has exactly five factors?

28 30 32 33

92 

Patterns and Functions

Professor Gizmo has created the Interdimensional Glickmeister Motor, which runs on rubbish—the more the better. With just $\frac{3}{4}$ of a pound of rubbish in the Converter Chamber, the motor produces 10 horsepower. Each additional pound of rubbish increases the production of the motor by 2.5 horsepower. List the horsepower produced by the following weights of trash:

3.75 pounds: ________________

5.75 pounds: ________________

7.75 pounds: ________________

Continue this pattern to determine how many pounds of trash are needed to generate 50 horsepower.

Daily Problems

93

Algebra

Use Base Ten Blocks.

If 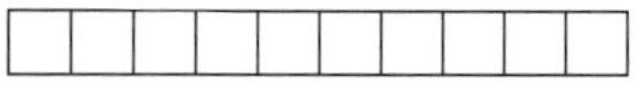 equals *x* and  equals 1, write an equation for the following:

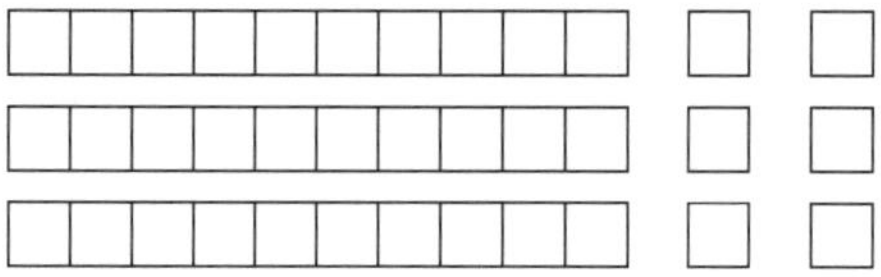

Draw two more groups of blocks and write the expression for each group.

94

Statistics

The table below shows the population density of several states. The density is measured by the number of people living in one square mile.

State	Population Density	State	Population Density
District of Columbia	9,743	Alaska	1
New Jersey	1,046	Wyoming	4.7
Rhode Island	961	Montana	5.6
Massachusetts	765	North Dakota	9.2
Connecticut	679	South Dakota	9.3

Chart these states on a map of the United States. What assumptions can you make about population density throughout the United States?

95

Measurement

Here are two facts to consider:

- A human being breathes approximately six quarts of air every minute.
- There are 14,625,000 people living in New York City.

How many *gallons* of air do New Yorkers consume in just one minute?

96

Geometry

Use a geoboard and rubber bands.

Can you form a scalene triangle inside an isosceles triangle?

Daily Problems

97

Probability

Use Color Tiles. Work with a partner.

Begin this quick game by giving your partner three Color Tiles: one red, one green, and one yellow. Ask your partner to arrange them in a certain order out of your sight. What is the probability that you will guess the order correctly the first time?

98

Logical Reasoning

Jerusha is walking through the forest with her rabbit, her cat, and her bird. Suddenly she comes to a wide river. Right by the shore there is a tiny rubber boat. The boat can hold only two of them. Jerusha can't leave the cat alone with the rabbit and she can't leave the cat alone with the bird. How many trips will she have to make across the river in the boat before she can get herself and all her pets to the other side?

Hint: Use a diagram to help solve this problem.

99

Numbers

Arlen has 95 cents. He has more quarters than dimes and more nickels than dimes. What coins could he have?

100

Patterns and Functions

Use Color Tiles or centimeter cubes.

Build a 1×1 square, a 2×2 square, a 3×3 square, and so on up to a 6×6 square. Record the number of tiles needed to make each square. Look for a pattern in the numbers. Describe the pattern.

How many tiles would be needed to build a 10×10 square? a 25×25 square?

Daily Problems

101

Algebra

Use centimeter cubes.

If the value of the cubes on the left side balances the value of the cubes on the right side, how many yellow cubes are equal to one brown cube?

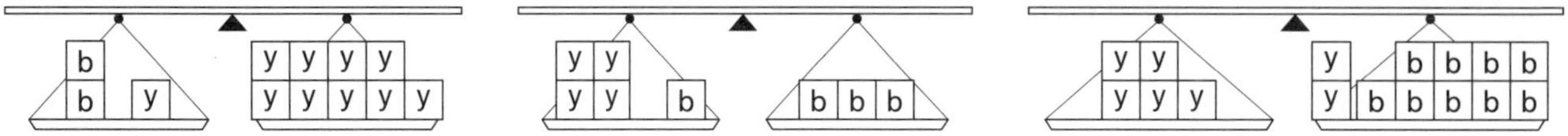

102

Statistics

Mr. Laroux, the principal at East Middle School, has decided to keep track of the amount of running in the corridors between classes. The chart below shows the number of students stopped for running at several locations in the school. Use this information to create a scatter chart.

	East Hall	Back Hallway	Front Corridor	Gymnasium Corridor	West Side Hall
Monday	26	12	41	55	9
Tuesday	16	7	32	48	9
Wednesday	15	7	25	32	7
Thursday	12	5	18	20	5
Friday	6	2	9	13	1

Where does the greatest amount of running in the hallways take place, given that the same number of students travel each area?

What effect is Mr. Laroux's enforcement of the no-running rule having schoolwide? Where has the enforcement had the greatest impact?

103 

Measurement

Barry Sanders of the Detroit Lions is one of the best rushers in the National Football League. In 1994 Sanders carried the football 331 times for an average of 5.7 yards each time. With this record, how many times did he carry the football the length of the field during the season?

104

Geometry

Use one set of tangram pieces.

Using just four tangram pieces, can you form a figure with two acute angles? Can you form a figure with no more than three right angles?

Daily Problems

105

Probability

It's true: The odds of finding a cracked egg in a shipment of eggs is 1 egg in 24 cartons *before* those cartons are placed on grocery store shelves. Once they are on shelves, however, your odds of getting a cracked egg rise to 1 egg in every 10 cartons. Each carton holds a dozen eggs. How many cracked eggs can a grocer expect to find in a shipment of 2,880 eggs just off the truck? How many more of these eggs will be cracked after being put on shelves? About what percent of the total shipment of eggs will be broken?

106 

Computation and Estimation

Six percent of the gasoline used by automobiles in the United States is burned while the cars are sitting in traffic jams. If the average car uses 480 gallons of gasoline a year, how many gallons does it burn in traffic jams? If the average price of a gallon of gas in 1995 was $1.40, how much money did the average car waste on gas burned in traffic jams?

107

Numbers

Only one of the following numbers is not a square of another number. Which is it?

16	9	64	49
36	25	4	100
13	81	144	121
9	169	81	4

108

Patterns and Functions

Use square grid or graph paper.

Officer McCarthy is about to go on patrol. She has a route she likes to follow, which you can trace on your grid paper. Place the station house roughly in the middle of the grid.

Upon leaving the station house, Officer McCarthy drives two blocks south, then turns and drives two blocks east. She turns again, this time driving three blocks north and then three blocks west. She turns again, driving two blocks south, then two blocks east. If she continues this pattern, will she ever drive past the station house?

Extra challenge: See what happens if Officer McCarthy increases the pattern by one, two, or three blocks in each direction.

Daily Problems

109

Algebra

⬡ − 6 < or = 7

What are all the numbers that could be written in ⬡ to make true sentences?

110

Computation and Estimation

Blindar the alien salesperson has opened a hotel in the Gorguuk galaxy. The total distance between the Gorguuk Resort and downtown Boston is 50,000,000 miles. If the space shuttle Blindar uses to transport guests from Boston to the hotel travels at 2,304 miles an hour, how many birthdays will a guest spend aboard the shuttle before arriving at the Gorguuk Resort?

111

Measurement

The moon is 238,900 miles from the Earth. The Sears Tower in Chicago is 1,454 feet tall. How many times would you have to stack the Sears Tower on top of itself to reach the moon?

112

Geometry

Use a geoboard and rubber bands.

Form each of the following triangles on the geoboard and record it on the dot array. Label each triangle.

- A right triangle (one angle that is 90° and two angles that are less than 90°)
- An obtuse triangle (one angle that is greater than 90° and two angles that are less than 90°)
- An acute triangle (three angles that are less than 90°)

Daily Problems

113

Logical Reasoning

Jody is at the Petting Zoo with her little sister. There are 29 rabbits and goats at the zoo. There are 21 goats and lambs running about, and 32 lambs and rabbits. How many of each kind of animal are at the Petting Zoo?

Hint: Use a Venn diagram to help solve this problem.

114

Numbers

The five members of the Zimbardo family love to play darts. At a recent family tournament, they scored a total of 350 points. Each person's score falls between 1 and 100. Each score is evenly divisible by 10. What are the five scores?

115

Patterns and Functions

Technology is making it possible for more and more television programs to be carried over a cable. In 1990, only 50 different stations could be carried on a cable. In 1992, that number had increased by 50%. In 1994, 75 more stations than the number in 1992 were able to be carried over a cable. Cable operators predict that in 1996 they will be able to carry twice as many stations as they did in 1994. If this pattern continues, how many stations will be able to be carried on cable at the turn of the century?

116 

Algebra

As C.B. looked through her binoculars at five rare Whistling Bixies, she also spotted 4 Red Hummers. The next day she saw 10 Bixies and 10 Hummers. On the third day she counted 15 Bixies and 14 Hummers. On the fourth day she saw 20 Bixies and 18 Hummers. If these patterns continue, on what day will C.B. see 10 more Bixies than Hummers? You may want to make a table like this to help solve the problem:

Day	1	2	3	
Bixies	5			
Hummers	4			

Daily Problems

117

Statistics

Here are two interesting facts: One out of every two Americans believes that life exists on other worlds, and 37% of Americans who did not attend college believe that there are extraterrestrial beings.

Write three true statements based on these two facts.

118

Measurement

Tea is a popular drink in Great Britain. The average citizen drinks 1,355 cups of tea annually. If a cup of tea holds approximately six fluid ounces and a barrel is equal to approximately 32 gallons, how many barrels of tea does one Englishperson drink in a year?

119

Geometry

Use Pattern Blocks.

The angles in the orange square are each 90 degrees. Together the angles add up to 360 degrees. Make three other polygons that each has angles adding up to 360 degrees.

120

Logical Reasoning

Over the years, many people have dressed up and run together in the Great Race as centipedes and spiders. Centipedes need seven people running together, and spiders need four people. In this year's race, there were 105 centipedes and spiders for a total of 1,230 racing legs. How many people were dressed as centipedes and how many were dressed as spiders?

Daily Problems

121

Computation and Estimation

Begin with the number of feet in one mile. Multiply that number by the number of weeks in a year. Now divide that number by the number of pints in a gallon. Do you think the answer will be more or less than 25,000? Estimate and then find the answer.

122

Patterns and Functions

Use Pattern Blocks.

Build each triangle shown. Then build the next three larger triangles. Record how many green blocks you used to build each triangle. Then write a rule that would tell someone how many blocks there would be in the 10th triangle.

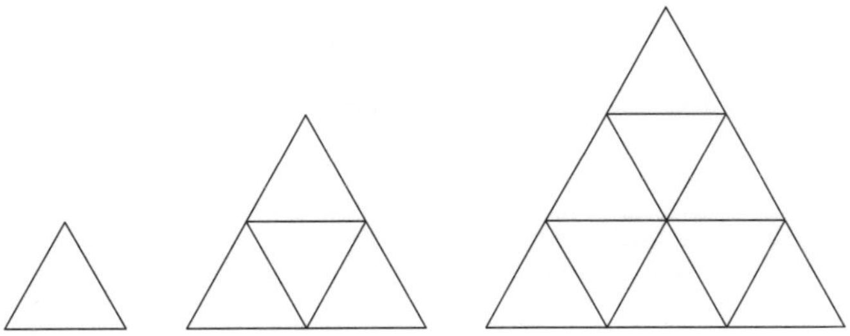

123

Measurement

Use a centimeter ruler or meter stick, string, and scissors. Work with a partner.

Stretch out your arms and estimate in centimeters the length of your armspan from finger tip to finger tip. Ask your partner to cut a string to match the length of your armspan. Measure the string in centimeters. Then estimate whether your height is less than or greater than the length of your string. Use your string to measure.

124

Geometry

The French Club wants to create a paper picture of the Eiffel Tower to hang on the side of the Midtown Bank as part of the city's American-French Sister City Program. The completed replica will actually be a triangle. If the base will be 10 yards wide and the top of the tower 60 yards high, what will be the total area of the paper tower expressed in feet?

Daily Problems

125

Statistics

It's a fact: Americans work about 6.2 more hours a week than they did in 1973. Assuming that the increase has been about the same each year, create a line graph that illustrates this increase, plotting the years 1975, 1980, 1985, 1990, and 1995.

126

Geometry

Use geometric solids.

Look at the prisms. How many faces, vertices, and edges does each prism have? Don't forget the ones you can't see in the pictures! Fill in the table. Describe the patterns you see in the numbers.

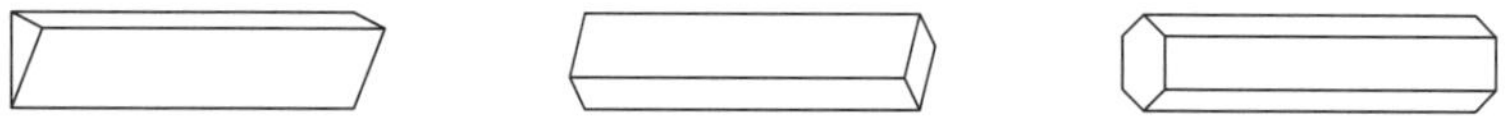

triangular prism   square prism   hexagonal prism

Prism	Sides of Base	Number of Faces	Number of Vertices	Number of Edges
triangular prism				
square prism				
hexagonal prism				

127

Patterns and Functions

Each day, Gregory's little brother Freddy gets an allowance. This is Freddy's allowance schedule: On the first Monday of the month, he is given one cent. Then his father doubles his allowance each day for the rest of the week. On the second Monday of the month he is given 2¢ and the amount doubles each day from the day before for six days. On the third Monday he is given 3¢ and the amount doubles each day for six days. On the fourth Monday he is given 4¢ and the amount doubles each day for six days. Gregory, on the other hand, gets an allowance of $2.50 a week. Which brother receives more allowance money by the end of four weeks and by how much?

128

Measurement

It's a fact: The average American consumes 3,642 calories daily. Just being alive burns about 100 calories an hour. If a person does no exercise for a year, how many unburned calories will he or she have at the end of the year? By how many calories could this person afford to reduce his or her diet without eating too few calories?

Daily Problems

129

Computation and Estimation

The science class built model rockets. Jay's rocket reached an altitude of 375 feet. Carla and Wilson's model reached an altitude 160% that of Jay's. T.C. and Kimiko built a larger rocket which, while moving faster, reached an altitude only $\frac{4}{5}$ that of Carla and Wilson's. List the altitude each team's rocket reached.

130

Patterns and Functions

Andy and Luis are trying to break the school record for jumping on a trampoline. The boys take turns jumping for an hour. Luis consistently makes 10% fewer jumps than Andy does. Andy increases the number of jumps he makes in an hour by 20 each time he jumps. During his first hour he jumped 200 times. Based on this, how many jumps did Luis make during his fifth hour on the trampoline?

131

Probability

Use a transparent spinner or a pencil and paper clip on the spinner shown. Work with a partner.

If you spin 20 times, what number do you predict the spinner will land on most often? Try it. Spin 20 times and record the results. Which number did the spinner land on most often?

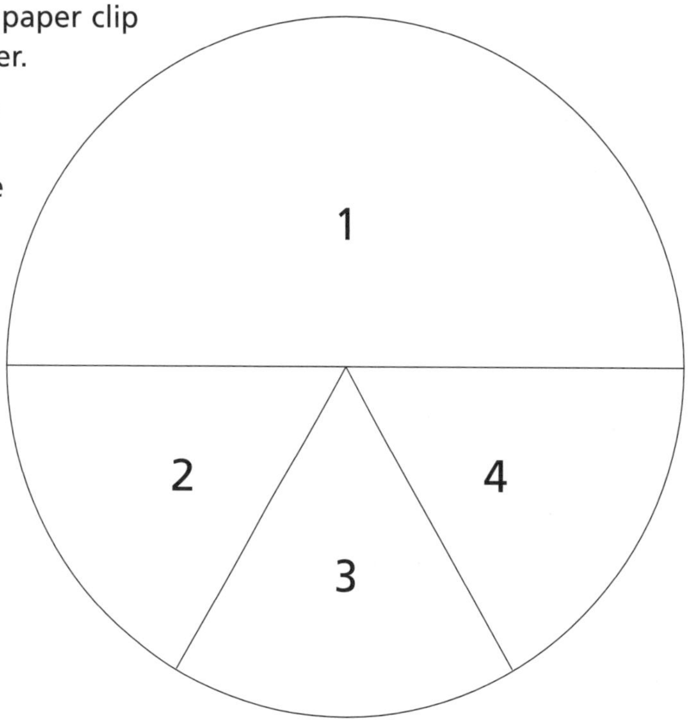

132

Measurement

Use centimeter cubes and a small box.

Estimate how many centimeter cubes will fill the box. Then put the cubes in the box. Record how many layers there are, how many cubes are in each layer, and how many cubes there are in all. Then figure out how long, how wide, and how high a box would be if 120 cubes filled it.

Daily Problems

133

Computation and Estimation

Gretchen and Katisha are working on the crime prevention campaign. They are painting reflective address numbers on the curbs in front of the houses in their neighborhood. Over the weekend the two girls painted a total of 2,000 digits. Each address is made up of four digits. How many complete address numbers did each girl paint if Katisha painted 50% more addresses than Gretchen?

134

Patterns and Functions

The military used to create alphanumeric codes to send messages across enemy lines. Can you figure out this code, which was actually sent at the end of the fighting?

18,46   18,8   42,22,26,24,22

Here is a hint: A = 26, B = 28, C = 24, D = 30, W = 4, X = 50, Y = 2, Z = 52.

135

Measurement

Trina and Mark have agreed to wash all of the windows on the Hannigans' greenhouse over the next few weeks. There are 4,000 panes of 1 foot × 3 feet glass in the greenhouse. Mr. Hannigan offered to pay 10¢ a square foot. Mark said he would rather get paid 30¢ a pane. Which way is the best deal for Trina and Mark?

136

Statistics

This graph shows the sorry state of Dave's savings account, which is now at $0. Use the pie graph to determine the ratio of money he spent on tickets for concerts and other entertainment to the money he spent for subscriptions to his favorite magazines. Then figure out the ratio of dollars spent on refreshments to dollars spent for tickets.

What percentage of the money was lost?

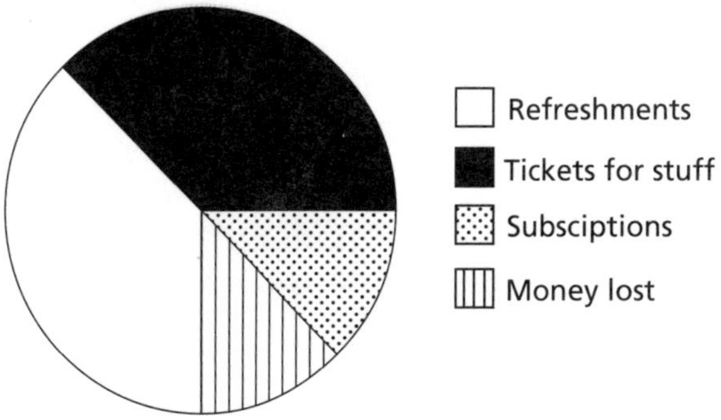

Daily Problems

137 

Computation and Estimation

Gargantuan Records is having a sale. If you buy five tapes or CDs, you receive a 10% discount on the total price. Each additional tape or CD adds another $\frac{1}{2}$% discount. How many tapes or CDs would you have to buy to receive a 15% discount on your total sale price? What would happen if you purchased 100 CDs? Would Gargantuan Records want to repeat this sale?

138

Geometry

The Cooking Club is planning to build a single pizza for the entire student body. If the radius of the pizza will be 4 ft, what will be the area of the top?

139 

Numbers

Compare the answers for each pair of problems. Are they different or are they the same?

A. ($^-6 \times 4$) and ($^-4 \times 6$)

B. ($^-6 \times {}^-4$) and (6×4)

C. ($24 \div {}^-6$) and ($24 \div 6$)

D. ($^-24 \div {}^-4$) and ($24 \div 4$)

140

Measurement

Use Color Tiles.

Mr. Hennesy is planning to cover part of the floor of the gym with stain-resistant square tiles before the science fair. Show all of the possible rectangular areas he can cover if he uses 60 tiles and there are no gaps between tiles. Which rectangular area has the longest perimeter? Which has the shortest perimeter?

Daily Problems

141

Statistics

As part of the annual Silly Sixth Grade Tricks Competition, Nate, Angelica, Mario, Li, and Christopher tried to fill the courtyard fountain in five minutes using only 12-ounce drinking cups. The table below illustrates the number of trips each student made from the barrel of water set up for this contest to the fountain.

Greg	Angelica	Mario	Li	Christopher
18	14	16	19	16

Write five questions about the activity that someone in your class can answer.

142

Probability

Use two regular 6-sided dice. Work with a partner if you can.

If you roll both dice 20 times, how often do you think you will roll two even numbers together? Make a prediction. Then try it. Roll both dice 20 times. Record the numbers you roll each time. Compare your results with your prediction. Are they close?

143

Logical Reasoning

Peter, Ann, Iko, and Latasha each have one pet: a dog, a cat, a parrot, and a snake. Use these clues and a diagram to decide who has which pet.

- Peter's pet calls him by name.
- Latasha is allergic to animal fur.
- Ann had to climb a tree last week to get her pet off a branch.

144

Algebra

Use Base Ten Blocks.

Use the blocks to make a rectangle that fits each expression. Draw the rectangle and record the blocks you used.

Example: 2(10 + 4) 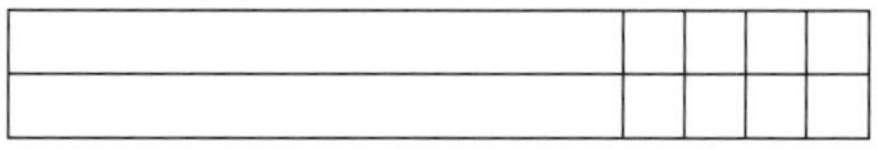 2 Tens, 8 Ones

3(10 + 9)

6(10 + 3)

Weekly Puzzlers

1 Rescue from Alpha Centauri

Computation and Estimation

Use a pair of regular 6-sided dice and a calculator.

Play this game with a partner. Roll the dice to see who plays first. The first player to roll a 5, or numbers that sum to 5, begins the game.

Imagine that you are 200 light-years away from a ship stranded on Alpha Centauri. The first player to reach the ship wins the game.

Take turns. On your turn, roll the dice and use both numerals. You may form a two-digit number, or you may add, subtract, multiply, or divide to get a score. Record your score in the tally chart.

Use a calculator to keep a running total of your scores. The first player who gets a total of exactly 200 is the winner.

Player 1		Player 2	
Score	Total	Score	Total

2 Mall Money

Algebra

Carol and Monica are spending the day at the mall. They began with $20.00 between them. Monica started out with $5.00 more than Carol, but spent twice as much as Carol. If, at the end of the day, Monica has $2.00 left, how much did Carol spend?

Write a new problem for Carol and Monica's day at the mall. Ask two algebra questions about your problem. Have a partner solve your problem.

Weekly Puzzlers

3 Can You Build to Scale?

Geometry

Use graph paper.

Leah and Latoya want to build a scale model of the Great Pyramid of Cheops. Each side of the base of the actual pyramid is 750 feet. The pyramid rises to a height of 450 feet. Use graph paper to create a scale drawing of the pyramid. You decide what measure a single square on the paper will have.

Can you also make scale drawings of some of the other wonders of the ancient world? (Here's a thought: The legs of the bronze statue known as the Colossus of Rhodes were taller than the tall ships that sailed at the time!)

---

4 Red's in Trouble!

Logical Reasoning

The newest store in the mall is a big hit: Red's Homemade Ice Cream. Red sells his "World's Finest" vanilla ice cream for \$10.00 a gallon, but for only \$7.00 a gallon if you buy more than four gallons. Red hired his neighbor, Floyd Processor, to write a computer program that will help Red keep track of sales and of his money. Unfortunately, Floyd made a few mistakes when he wrote the program. As a result, the steps of the program are not in the correct sequence.

Read the following commands and rearrange them so that the program makes sense. The first two lines are in their proper positions.

001 Enter x, the total number of gallons being sold to the customer.

002 If $x > 4$, then skip the next three commands. If $x <$ or $= 4$, proceed to the next line.

003 Multiply $(x - 4)$ by \$7.00. The result $= a$.

004 Multiply b by 0.07. The result $= c$.

005 Add $a + \$40.00$. The result $= b$.

006 Multiply x by \$10.00. The result $= y$.

007 Add $y + z$. Print the total and end the program.

008 Multiply y by 0.07. The result $= z$.

009 Add $b + c$. Print the total and end the program.

Now that you are an expert at arranging code, write your own programs to perform simple mathematical tasks.

Weekly Puzzlers

5 Floor Plan

Patterns and Functions

Use Color Tiles and square grid paper.

You have 50 Color Tiles that you must use to create two unique floor plans for a new music store. Use all 50 tiles to create each floor plan. The only rule you must follow is: At least one side of a tile must completely touch the side of another tile. For example:

This is acceptable. 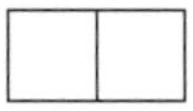

This is not acceptable. 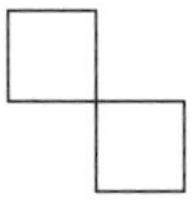

Sketch your floor plans on the grid paper. Beside each plan, give the measurement of the plan's perimeter.

6 Aliens Ate My Breakfast!

Numbers

You and the other members of your class have been asked to play the part of a hysterical mob in the upcoming movie "Aliens Ate My Breakfast." Unfortunately, there are only 26 people in your class and the director wants a mob of 500 people. To solve the problem, the costume department has brought in a dozen each of shirts, pants, skirts, dresses, shorts, and tops for you and your classmates to change into and out of. The director will then film you wearing different clothes. Are there enough clothes to make it look like 500 different people are running through the building? How many times will each of you have to change some or all of your costume?

Make up your own "Aliens Ate My Breakfast" problem. Have a partner solve your problem.

Weekly Puzzlers

7 There Are Numbers in Those Numbers

Numbers

Everywhere we look, in everything we read, and everywhere we go, there are numbers. You already know that there are 7 days in a week and that 7 is a prime number. You also know that a quarter equals 25 cents and that 25 is a square number. How many other prime and square numbers can you find in daily life?

Numbers in Daily Life

Prime Numbers	Square Numbers

8 Who Are the Heroes?

Probability

According to the Harris Poll, the chance a child's hero will be an actor is 2 in 5, an athlete 1 in 10, and a politician 1 in 16. Conduct your own survey. Ask 20 kids, chosen at random, to name their number one hero. What does your survey show? Were the chances the same as in the Harris Poll?

Weekly Puzzlers

9 A Hexomino Happening

Geometry

Use Color Tiles.

A hexomino is a shape made of six squares connected by one or more entire sides. The illustration below is a hexomino that can be made into a box if it is drawn on paper and the sides folded up. Not all hexomino designs can be made into boxes. How many different hexomino shapes can you make that can be traced on paper and then folded into boxes? Create several boxes and ask your friends to build them.

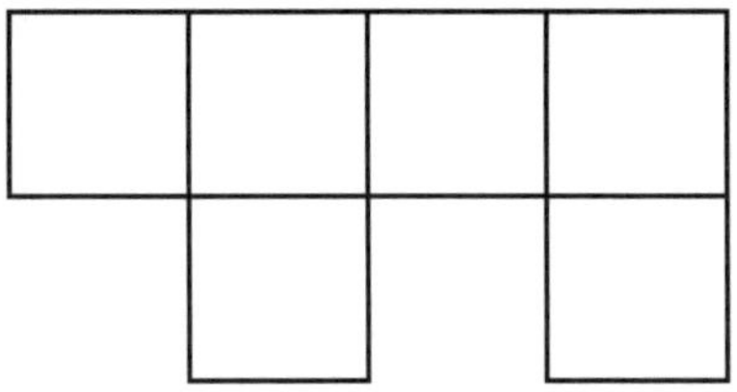

10 Who's Sitting Where?

Logical Reasoning

It's Thanksgiving! Maria, her sister, brother, mother, father, grandmother, grandfather, Uncle Bart, and friends Mr. and Mrs. Lopez are sitting down to dinner. Use the following clues to help you find out where everyone is sitting at the table. Each person is facing the table.

- The table is a rectangle.
- Maria's mother and father sit at each end of the table.
- Every male is sitting between two females.
- Maria's father is sitting next to two of his children.
- Maria is sitting next to her father and someone not in her family.
- Maria's grandfather is sitting next to a granddaughter and someone not in the family.
- Maria's brother sits to the left of his mother and across from Uncle Bart.

Make up your own "dinner table" logic problem. Put from 6 to 12 people at the table.

Weekly Puzzlers

11 Pattern Builder

Patterns and Functions

Use Pattern Blocks.

Begin with one blue rhombus. Add blue blocks to make the next larger, similar rhombus. Hint: Double the length of every side of the first rhombus. Record how many blocks it takes to make the second rhombus. Keep adding blue blocks to make larger, similar shapes. Record in the table.

Then try the orange squares and make larger squares. Next use the green triangles. Try making larger triangles.

	Sides × 1 Blocks	Sides × 2 Blocks	Sides × 3 Blocks	Sides × 4 Blocks	Sides × 5 Blocks
◇	1	4			
△	1				
□	1				

Describe any patterns you see in your table.

12 You Be the Producer

Computation and Estimation

You have been hired to be the producer of an evening news show. The program is scheduled to run for precisely 30 minutes. It must include at least five commercial breaks, none of which can be the same length of time as any other. Additionally, the sports must be three minutes longer than the weather, and the weather section must be shorter than the "hard news" section. You must also allow five minutes in the program for what is called "happy talk," where the newscasters talk to one another about almost anything.

Use this information to chart out all the time periods that must make up the program. Make a chart like the one started below, broken into 30-second sections. Compare your completed chart with an actual 30-minute evening news program.

0:00	
0:30	
1:00	
1:30	
2:00	
2:30	

Weekly Puzzlers

13 The Path Home

Numbers

Write numbers in this maze. Make a path of prime numbers from the Start to the Turnaround and a path of numbers that are squares of some other numbers from the Turnaround back to the Start. Fill in a few trick numbers, too. Then give your maze to a friend and see if your friend can follow your path of primes and squares.

14 New Shape City

Geometry

Use several sets of tangrams.

Imagine a city built entirely from new and unusual shapes. Now create a structure in this city using your tangram pieces. Determine the area of the building if the small triangle is equal to 2 units of area. Create a library, a government building, a bank, and two stores of your choice.

Weekly Puzzlers

15 Summer Survey

Statistics

The 24-member Student Council is trying to decide how the school should use the available money to celebrate the beginning of summer:

- Six members want to hold a school dance.
- Five members want to have an old-fashioned barbecue.
- Four members want to buy an all-school pass to the amusement center.
- Five members want to hold a carnival.
- Four members want to divide the money up equally among the classes and let each class sponsor decide.

Express this information in three different graphical forms.

Conduct your own survey. Find out how your friends and classmates would like to celebrate the beginning of summer.

16 Can You Get Here from There?

Measurement

Here is a perplexing problem: Your friend is standing just 10 feet away from you. You ask her to move forward, covering half the distance that separates you. Then you ask her to do the same thing again. Has she reached you? How many feet has your friend covered? How many feet will she have covered by the time she has moved 10 times?

Repeat the problem with another friend and another distance. Use a yardstick measure.

Weekly Puzzlers

17 Pattern Pie

Patterns and Functions

Can you find the pattern in the numbers on this wheel? Explain the pattern. Then create your own pattern wheel and challenge a friend to find the pattern.

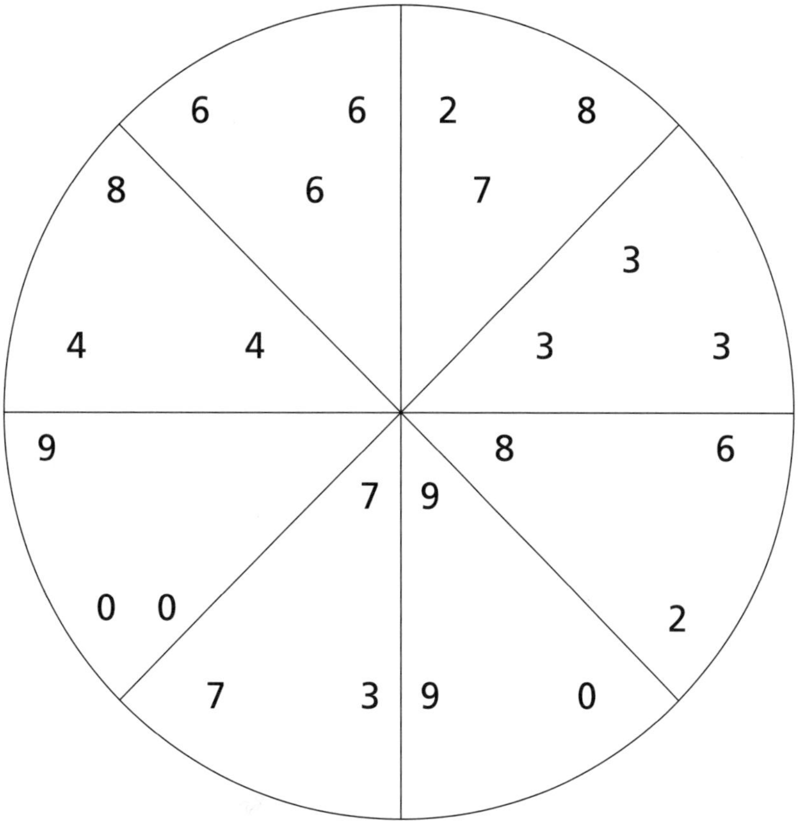

18 Bread and Water

Algebra

It's a fact: It takes 100 gallons of water to make a loaf of bread! Water must be used to grow and grind the wheat; to process the salt, baking powder, and any flavorings in the bread; and to add to the batter.

For each loaf of bread, the batter requires 0.5 of a gallon of water. Growing and processing the flavorings require four times the amount of water needed for grinding the wheat, which is eight times the amount of water required in the batter. How much water is needed to grow and process the flavorings? Let this number equal F. Let the amount of water needed to grind the wheat equal G. The amount of water needed to process the salt is equal to $(0.25F) + 2$. How much water is needed to process the salt? Let this number equal S.

How many gallons of water are required to grow the wheat for one loaf of bread?

Weekly Puzzlers

19 Count Up

Probability

Use centimeter cubes and a paper bag.

In this activity, you will see how difficult it can be to get four of anything! Place five red, five green, five yellow, and five blue cubes in a bag. Without looking inside the bag, draw out four cubes. Score your draws like this:

1 of each color	=	100 points
2 of the same color and 2 of another color	=	10,000 points
3 of the same color and 1 of another color	=	1,000 points
4 of the same color	=	100,000 points

What is your total score after five draws? Try this again. How does your score compare to the first time? What do you think your score would be like if you did this again?

20 Dream Week

Measurement

Use a map of your state.

A wonderful aunt comes to visit for one week. She loves to see everything and has never been to your state before. Use the map scale to figure out how many different places you can visit in one week if you travel a maximum of 500 miles a day beginning from your city. Use a linear measure from location to location; don't worry about any curves in the road.

Be sure to allow time to explore some of the places you visit.

Weekly Puzzlers

21 If I Could Change Time

Computation and Estimation

On weekdays, how much time do you spend in school, doing homework, watching television, eating, and sleeping? Find out by keeping track of your time from 8:00 a.m. on Monday to 8:00 p.m. on Friday.

	School	Homework	Television	Eating	Sleeping
Monday					
Tuesday					
Wednesday					
Thursday					
Friday					
Total Time					

Now, think about what would happen if the amount of time you spent eating doubled? Would it be more or less than the amount of time you spent watching television? What if you attended school for twice the amount of time you spent watching television and $1\frac{1}{2}$ times the amount of time you spent sleeping? Would that be more or less time than you usually spend in school?

Now, write one of your own "What if?" questions. Answer it for yourself, then ask a friend to answer it.

22 The Sporting Life

Statistics

Sports are a great way to have fun and get lots of exercise, too. Conduct a survey of at least 10 kids, asking each for his or her three favorite sports. Assemble the data and create three graphs: first preference, second preference, and third preference. What similarities and patterns do you note in the three graphs? Explain your findings to the class.

Weekly Puzzlers

23 Who Says You Need a Ruler?

Measurement

Did you know that you can measure just about anything with a penny? The diameter of a penny is approximately $\frac{3}{4}$ of an inch. You can also measure anything with a quarter or a dollar. Find out the length of a dollar bill and the diameter of a quarter. Now figure out how much it costs to walk the distance from your desk to the drinking fountain (or any place in the room) using pennies, quarters, and dollar bills as your measuring tools.

24 Ten in One

Computation and Estimation

Mrs. Dayton's sixth-grade math students are writing their own book of story problems for students to solve. They decided not to write separate story problems but to write a one-paragraph story that would give all the information needed to solve ten problems.

Try your hand at it! Make your story imaginative and fun! Write ten problems that can be solved using the information given in your story. Record your solutions to the problems on a separate sheet of paper. Then give your story and ten problems to a partner to solve.

Weekly Puzzlers

25 Big, Bigger, Biggest

Computation and Estimation

Use three regular 6-sided dice.

This game is for three players. Each of you will need a chart like the one shown below. On the first round, each of you rolls the die four times. After each roll, enter the number rolled as a digit in the first row of your chart. You may place the number in the thousands, hundreds, tens, or ones column; but you may not move it once you have placed it. After all of you have completed your four-digit numbers, compare the numbers. The player with the largest number on that round stars his or her number. Play nine more rounds. The player who has the most starred numbers after ten rounds is the winner.

	Four-Digit Number				
Round	**Thousands**	**Hundreds**	**Tens**	**Ones**	*
1					
2					
3					
4					
5					
6					
7					
8					
9					
10					

26 Prime Time

Numbers

Use a hundred chart.

A prime number is a number that is divisible only by itself and 1. List all the prime numbers less than 100.

Twin prime numbers are any two prime numbers that differ only by 2, for example, 3 and 5. How many twin primes can you find? How many triplets?

Weekly Puzzlers

27 What's the Relationship?

Logical Reasoning

Study these analogies. Find the relationship and then supply the missing information.

Base $\times$ height : rectangle as ________________ : triangle

Octahedron : 8 as dodecahedron : ________________

Angle $>$ 90° : obtuse as ________________ : acute

4 quarts : 1 gallon as ________________ : 1 quart

Now, create five of your own analogies.

28 All Wrapped Up

Geometry

Use geometric solids (or objects that have the shapes of solids), blank paper or newspaper, scissors, and tape.

The artist Cristo is famous for wrapping things—buildings, bridges, even entire mountain tops.

Following in Cristo's footsteps, wrap a geometric solid. Begin by estimating the amount and shape of paper you will need to completely wrap the solid. Then cut the wrapping out of the paper and put it around the solid. How close was your estimate? Try the same thing with other geometric solids.

Weekly Puzzlers

29 Sum Table

Computation and Estimation

Can you complete this table with the numbers 4 through 8 so that no row or column has two of the same number? Does every completed row and column have the same sum? After you complete the table, make up a similar problem and give it to a friend to solve.

8	4	6	5	7
				5
				6
				8
				4

30 Where in the World?

Measurement

Use a globe. Work with a partner if you can.

Did you know that you can locate places in the world if you use the grid of lines on a globe? Lines of latitude circle the globe and run parallel to the equator. Lines of longitude run from the North Pole to the South Pole. Latitude and longitude are measured in degrees. Look at the globe and find measurements written in degrees on the grid lines.

Latitude is measured both north and south from the equator, which is the 0-degree line of latitude. About how many degrees north of the equator is the city of Rome, Italy? About how many degrees north of the equator is your home?

Longitude is measured both east and west from the line of longitude that runs through Greenwich, England, which is the 0-degree line of longitude. About how many degrees west of Greenwich is Miami, Florida? About how many degrees west of Greenwich is your home?

Describe the location of a "mystery" city. Use the lines of latitude and longitude on the globe to describe the location. Be sure to tell how many degrees north or south the city is from the equator, and how many degrees east or west the city is from Greenwich.

Weekly Puzzlers

31 Festival Float

Algebra

The school band is trying to raise money to build a float for the Festival Parade. The students have decided to collect recyclable trash and then sell it to a local recycling company. They can earn 2.5¢ per pound for cardboard, 3¢ per pound for newspaper, and 55¢ per pound for aluminum. How many pounds of each material must they collect to earn the $300 they need for a float if they collect twice as much aluminum as cardboard?

Contact your nearest recycling center and find out the current price they pay for cardboard, newspaper, aluminum, and glass. Write your own problem about recycling for another student to solve.

32 Going Vertical

Geometry

Most of you have places where you like to meet with your friends after school and on weekends. Lines like to meet at the vertex. The letter A has two lines meeting at its vertices, as shown below:

vertex ⟶ A ⟵ vertex

Print your name. Below each letter, note the number of lines that meet at the vertices of the letter. Compare the number of vertices in your name with those in the names of friends.

Weekly Puzzlers

33 Red Shirt Day

Probability

Make a chart that describes the shirt colors, shoe colors, hair colors, or any other distinguishing characteristic you choose, for all the kids in your class. Keep this record on your desk. Use it to answer these questions:

1. According to your chart, what is the probability that the first person to get out of his or her seat at a certain time (10:00 a.m., for example) will be wearing the color red?
2. According to your chart, what is the probability that the last person to leave the room for lunch will be wearing the color brown?

After answering the questions, use your chart to write and answer four probability questions of your own.

34 House of Cards

Geometry

Use playing cards, a measuring tape, and graph paper.

Here is a challenge for you and a partner. Use a deck of playing cards to construct the largest, greatest structure you can—without using tape. Measure the structure's height, length, and area, and then draw a blueprint of it on graph paper.

Weekly Puzzlers

35 The Angle of Time

Measurement

Use a clock and a protractor.

The two hands of a clock form angles. Check the clock five times during the day, and fill in the chart below.

Time	Approximate Measurement of Angle Between Hour and Minute Hands	Type of Angle

36 Whether or Not There Is Weather (or Not!)

Probability

Every day, meteorologists predict what the weather will be in your area. They use radar, past records, and current weather to help them make accurate predictions. How accurate a prediction can you make using just your own senses? Make a chart and record on it your meteorologist's prediction for tomorrow's weather and your own. Continue for a total of 10 days. At the end of 10 days, compare your prediction accuracy with that of the meteorologist.